I LIVED TO TELL IT ANTHOLOGY VOL. 2

MY STORY
HIS TESTIMONY
THE POWER OF
FORGIVENESS

AND THEY OVERCAME HIM BY THE BLOOD OF THE LAMB, AND BY THE WORD OF THEIR TESTIMONY; AND THEY LOVED NOT THEIR LIVES UNTO THE DEATH.
—REVELATION 12:11

DR. TINA M. BEATTY **VISIONARY AUTHOR**

© 2024 Dr. Tina M. Beatty

Book Cover Design: Auther Perdue - AP Media Solutions
Interior Book Design & Formatting: TamikaINK.com
Editor: TamikaINK.com

ALL RIGHTS RESERVED. No part of this book may be reproduced in any written, electronic, recording, or photocopying without written permission of the publisher or author. The exception would be in the case of brief quotations embodied in critical articles or reviews and pages where permission is specifically granted by the publisher or author.

LEGAL DISCLAIMER. Although the author has made every effort to ensure that the information in this book was correct at press time, the author does not assume hereby disclaim any liability to any party for loss, damage, or disruption caused by errors or missions, whether such errors or omissions result from negligence, accident, or any other cause.

Published By: Igniting The Flame Publishing

Library of Congress Cataloging-in-Publication Data has been applied for

ISBN: 9798324735340

PRINTED IN THE UNITED STATES OF AMERICA

Table of Contents

FOREWORD IN A POEM: FORGIVE AND BE FORGIVEN
BY PROFESSOR TIERRA D. GRAVES, M.ED 5

INTRODUCTION 9

CHAPTER 1: I FORGIVE ME BY DR. TINA M. BEATTY.................... 12

CHAPTER 2: CHOOSING FORGIVENESS: THE DISCOVERY AND
REDEMPTION OF A FATHER-DAUGHTER RELATIONSHIP
BY EVANGELIST LYNN L. KING... 27

CHAPTER 3: UNRAVELING THE LAYERS OF A SPIRITUAL ONION
BY PROPHET MATTIE MORGAN 39

CHAPTER 4: INCLINED TO FORGIVE BY APRIL BATTLE................ 51

CHAPTER 5: HOW CAN YOU BE A DAUGHTER TO A STRANGER?
BY MARIAN B. JONES-ALLEN 61

CHAPTER 6: WHY ME, GOD? BY PROPHET CARLOTTA LYNCH 73

CHAPTER 7: THE REBIRTHING – BEHOLD, I AM DOING
SOMETHING NEW BY APOSTLE MICHELLE FRANKLIN 83

CHAPTER 8: GET FREED TO SET FREE BY MINISTER SAMANTHA
STANLEY.. 91

CHAPTER 9: FORGIVING THEM WHO HURT YOU AND THEY NEVER
KNEW BY PASTOR KATHY CLARK... 101

CHAPTER 10: THE MIRACLE OF FORGIVING
BY PASTOR ROSLYN WILLIAMS 113

CHAPTER 11: TO FORGIVE OR NOT TO FORGIVE?
BY TUNISIA K. BEATTY 121

CHAPTER 12: I HAVE FORGIVEN YOU
BY NORMA NANETTE HINES 131

CHAPTER 13: THE VOICE BY NICHELLE A. TRIGGS ROBINSON 143

FORGIVENESS HANDBOOK BY DR. TINA M. BEATTY

31-DAY FORGIVENESS SCRIPTURE PLAN 155

THE HOW, WHY, WHAT, WHERE, WHEN, AND WHO TO FORGIVE
.... 157

ACKNOWLEDGMENTS

SPECIAL THANKS BY CO-AUTHORS 169

FOREWORD IN A POEM
Forgive and Be Forgiven
By Professor Tierra D. Graves, M.Ed.

Plethora of unforgiveness sweeping the nation
Enlighten in error so forgiveness displaced.
Or was the truth misused?
As we walk in misconduct
With resentment towards others.
Wrongdoing was done but does it destroy or deploy.
To submit to refuse a pardon?
Causes such dishonor.
Whether you or others
Unforgiveness has swallowed you up.
In disbelief we disagree with the offense
Life around us intense
Years of resentment
Only God heal this, through repentance.
Dance around the idea to forgive.
Until it's the only choice, to live!
Behind the marked heart
Memories fade into the distance.
As we witness God's forgiveness is evidence

PROFESSOR TIERRA D. GRAVES, M.ED.

Dearth the necessity to forgive thee,
Life lessons learned to rest and release.
Annoyance no longer in bondage
Illuminate through prayer and God's word.
The power of forgiveness
A reflection of God's love
Forgive and be forgiven!

Tierra Graves

Tierra Graves was born in Washington, DC but currently resides in Maryland. After graduating from Eastern Senior High School in Washington DC with honors, she spent several years studying in college. She currently holds a bachelor's degree in English with a minor in Education from Trinity Washington University. She also holds a master's degree in Secondary Education, Secondary Humanities Education from Grand Canyon University. Ms. Graves also completed a summer course where she received a certificate/license from Goucher College to teach Advanced Placement Courses on the secondary level for English coursework. On April 7, 2024, she received a certificate/license from World TESOL Academy to teach English as a Second Language.

Ms. Graves is a 6-time published author. She published *Prism of Me, A New Twist on Old Traditions, A New Twist on Old Traditions Workbook,* and *Depression Before Tea: Journey A to Z* with Christian Living Books, Inc. She later published, *I Lived to Tell It Testimonial Anthology, alongside of 11 women of God as a Co-Author* with In Due Seasons Publishing Company. Her bonus book, *The Record,* was published with Trinity Washington University.

Ms. Graves has taught English for grades 6-12 with District of Columbia Public Schools for the past six years. She has also taught Biology, Art, and Spanish courses on the middle and high school levels. Currently she works as an Adjunct Professor at the University of the Potomac teaching ESL-English as a Second Language and English Composition Courses. Ms. Graves writes poetry, short stories, essays and so much more. She is a dedicated member of Household of Faith Ministries where she has been under the leadership of Bishop and Pastor Jones since 2012. Her relationship with God is her strength. She is a motivational speaker and liturgical dancer where she uses her testimony of overcoming obstacles to uplift and inspire others through her relationship with the Lord and the word of God.

Introduction

By Dr. Tina M. Beatty

"Let all bitterness, and wrath, and anger, and clamour, and evil speaking, be put away from you, with all malice: and be ye kind one to another, tenderhearted, forgiving one another, even as God for Christ's sake hath forgiven you." Ephesians 4:32 KJV

Who do you need to pardon? What has caused you to neglect forgiving yourself and others? When did you realize you were living with unforgiveness in your heart? Why have you allowed unforgiveness to control your life and hinder you from walking in your full potential? Where were you the moment you accepted the opportunity to excuse yourself and others? How do you plan to acquit yourself and others to live the life Christ designed for you? Reflect on these questions and come along with us on this journey to forgiveness.

These questions are examples of what resonates in our hearts and spirits, beckoning us to examine ourselves and the people around us. According to Merriam-Webster, to be unforgiving means having or making no allowance for error or weakness and/or being unwilling or unable to excuse. In addition, forgiveness is the act of ceasing to feel resentment against an offender. According to God's Word, forgiveness means, *"Make allowance for each other's faults and forgive anyone who offends you. Remember, the Lord forgave you, so you must forgive others"* (Colossians 3:13 NLT).

My Story, His Testimony, The Power of Forgiveness, is a collection of testimonial stories where each author explores moments of bitterness, wrath, anger, and so much more to embrace forgiveness in their lives. Consider the thought that your story is what happened to you, but His testimony is what God did through you because of the offense.

This book will take you through a journey of discovery and honest reflection to embark on the tender heart of overcoming unforgiveness at the most pivotal moments in one's life. The guiding force of God's Word commands us to forgive. The power of forgiveness that can be achieved when we obey His voice is witnessed through each story. The testimony of Christ states in His Word that He has forgiven us. Therefore, if he has forgiven us of all wrongdoings, we are to do the same for all people.

Your full purpose in life will be manifested once you decide to forgive and proclaim the glory of the Lord. Each author is a witness and can testify that unexpected blessings manifested when they needed them most because of their obedience to forgive. For in doing so, we uncover the power of forgiveness and announce God's testimony, which makes room for others to be inspired, encouraged, and healed because *I Lived to Tell It.*

You will read overcoming testimonies of how God allowed each author to make allowances for and stop feeling resentment toward themselves and others in the most powerful ways that brought healing and deliverance. The purpose of this book is to bring awareness and hope around forgiveness as we believe God has no respect of person, and what He did for us, He can do for you if you open your heart and make room for God to come in.

In ordinary moments, God can use anyone to help transform the narrative of unforgiveness. Are you ready to tell of the power of forgiveness in your life? Were you taught in error? You have been holding on to unforgiveness for too long; it is time to release it. Thus, *"...if you refuse to forgive others, your Father will not forgive your sins" (Matthew 6:15 NLT).*

The undeniable presence of God can guide you through the power of forgiveness. *My Story, His Testimony, The Power of Forgiveness* is a book that heals.

CHAPTER 1
I Forgive Me
By Dr. Tina M. Beatty

Forgiveness is a gift you give yourself.
~ Suzanne Somers

Forgiveness is God's command.
~ Martin Luther

It's one of the greatest gifts you can give yourself, to forgive. Forgive everybody.
~ Maya Angelou

Have you ever gone to someone and asked them to forgive you because of something you said or done, to find out later they didn't receive it? Well, this is my story; there have been many times in my life when I have offended or wronged someone, knowingly and unknowingly, intentionally and unintentionally, and I had to go back to that person and ask them for forgiveness.

Even as believers in Jesus Christ, it is not always easy to do, especially when they have offended you as well. There are many valid reasons why you shouldn't, but the Word of God commands us to FORGIVE.

His Testimony:

In Mark 11:25-26 KJV *And when ye stand praying, forgive, if ye have ought against any: that your Father also which is in heaven may forgive you your trespasses. But if ye do not forgive, neither will your Father which is in heaven forgive your trespasses.* This scripture, among other scriptures in the Bible, explains how important it is to our Heavenly Father to forgive because it's not about the other person but about you being obedient to the word of God.

When you forgive, it reveals the healed condition of your heart because it will speak, just as with an unforgiving heart, it will speak it, too. It can't be quiet; it wants to prove a point by being right about how it feels. Having unforgiveness in your heart will have you play the victim, be defensive, have angry outbursts, put a guilt trip on you, or shift the blame off of them onto you to make you feel like it's your fault because it's never theirs. I'm not saying this because this is as if I don't know; I know because I've been on both sides of the coin, forgiveness and unforgiveness.

O generation of vipers, how can ye, being evil, speak good things? for out of the abundance of the heart the mouth speaketh. A good man out of the good treasure of the heart bringeth forth good things: and an evil man out of the evil treasure bringeth forth evil things. But I say unto you, That every idle word that men shall speak, they shall give account thereof in the day of judgment. Matthew 12:34-36 KJV

Forgiveness bringeth forth good things whether you realize it or not; it's always good because it's God; the devil is not going to tell you to forgive; he's going to tell you not to forgive a person because of what they said, did and how they hurt your feelings. So we need to know the difference between who's voice we are listening to and obeying, especially when we are going through.

And when he putteth forth his own sheep, he goeth before them, and the sheep follow him: for they know his voice. And a stranger will they not follow, but will flee from him: for they know not the voice of strangers. John 10:4-5

So, withholding forgiveness from anyone or about anything is not an option. It is a command, mandatory, essential, absolutely necessary, and a powerful weapon against the enemy. So, I choose to forgive across the board because I need that same grace and mercy extended to me if or when I sin. I understand the power of forgiveness, and it will work for me and it will work for you.

FORGIVE, verb transitive forgiv'. preterit tense forgave; participle passive forgiven. [Latin remitto. See Give.]
1. To pardon; to remit, as an offense or debt; to overlook an offense; and treat the offender as not guilty. The original and proper phrase is to forgive the offense, send it away, reject it, and not to impute it, [put it to] the offender. But by an easy transition, we also use the phrase to forgive the person offending.

Forgiveness
FORGIV'ENESS, noun forgiv'ness.
1. Forgiveness is the act of pardoning an offender, by which he is considered and treated as not guilty.
Forgiveness of enemies is a Christian duty.
2. The pardon or remission of an offense or crime, as the forgiveness of sin or of injuries.
3. Disposition to pardon; willingness to forgive.
And mild forgiveness intercedes to stop the coming blow.
4. Remission of a debt, fine, or penalty. King James Bible Dictionary - Reference List - Forgive

As I get back to my story, there was a time in 2017 when I and a friend disagreed, and we quit speaking. It was like six months to a year that went by when we didn't see each other again. But when God was working on me, I would seek His face by praying, repenting, asking for forgiveness, and reading His word daily. This prepared me ahead of time for whenever the day came for us to talk again.

So that day finally came, and I asked her how she was doing. We began to talk, and it was then that I asked her to forgive me for what I said to her; she accepted it, or so I thought. And the reason I said so, I thought, is because when I saw her again, she started to bring it back up again what happened. I said wait a minute. I came to you and asked for forgiveness. I thought we were past that, but I guess not.

So, needless to say, the conversation ended, and we both walked away. But then there was another time I saw her again with her friends, and she brought it up again, and I thought to myself, here we go again. I knew it was time to go, so I left and got into my car. I began to talk to the Lord about what happened, so I started to pray and cry out to the Lord right in my car because I didn't want to relive the situation every time I came in contact with her. I know what I said was wrong, I know I may have hurt your feelings, and I know you were offended you but wasn't forgiveness enough? And that's when I heard the Holy Spirit say to me, "Don't let other people's unforgiveness towards you keep you in bondage! You obeyed my word; now go to the next level of forgiveness and forgive yourself, and keep moving. Don't become like them or go; keep moving."

Forgive yourself for your faults and your mistakes, and move on.
~ Les Brown
As we know, the forgiveness of oneself is the hardest of all the forgiveness.
~ Joan Baez

When I heard that, I said to myself, "I FORGIVE ME, I FORGIVE ME! I've forgiven everybody else. I've even asked for their forgiveness, but I forgot to forgive myself."

I tried my best to make sure I walked in love and forgiveness, that my heart was right towards the person or persons, not holding any grudges or being bitter. Now that I know I didn't give the same grace, mercy, and forgiveness to myself that I gave to others, the trajectory of my life changed. Because I began to see things differently when it came to me, I didn't allow how someone felt or thought about me to affect me anymore; it doesn't bother me anymore because people can stay where they are if that's what they choose. I refuse to be held hostage to anyone's unforgiveness, bitterness, control, emotional breakdown, or even their words. I choose to FORGIVE QUICKLY!

The speed of your forgiveness reveals the health of your heart!
~ Prophet Kudzai Muskwe

So, the word "no" became easier to say because I understood how important it was to have peace if I didn't want to do it; I didn't have to. Self-care allowed me to take care of myself in a way that removed the excess baggage I carried from other people that wasn't mine to carry.

Once I realized I could forgive myself, the scales fell off my eyes. Forgiveness can break any and all strongholds, heal the sick, bring forth deliverance, and set souls free. It can restore relationships, reconcile, and prevent further harm, damage, or suffering. It is a powerful weapon against the enemy.

Recently, I was faced with many challenges concerning my health. I needed to see my family doctor to find out what was wrong because I was in so much pain at work with my back, hips, spine, and neck, and migraines. So I went, and they ran all kinds of tests on me. They told me my cholesterol was high; I had bulging disks, degenerative joint disease, radiculopathy, arthritis, and osteoarthritis.

After I received the results, I began to pray, and the Holy Spirit reminded me about a book I had: A More Excellent Way, Be in Health, Spiritual Roots of Disease Pathways to Wholeness by Henry W. Wright. I began to read up on all that was told to me to find out the spiritual root of what was going on in my body. And I'm sharing this because we as believers need to get to the root of the matter so that we can know what to pray and how to pray while using the scriptures in the Bible to uproot, tear down, break the powers of it, cast it out, decree and declare the Word of the Lord to receive healing and everything that concerns us.

- On page 280 by Henry W. Wright ... migraines are triggered in people who have conflict with themselves about conflict in life or conflict with others. It is rooted in guilt. All migraines are rooted in guilt. Out of guilt comes fear, and it is always in this order. It is guilt first and then fear.

• On page 262 by Henry W. Wright ... cholesterol is directly related to people who are very angry with themselves. There is a high degree of self-depreciation deprecation; they are against themselves and always putting themselves down. It is more than merely putting themselves down; they are very hostile to themselves. They are very angry with themselves.

• On page 240, Henry W. Wright describes arthritis as inflammation of the joints. Basic simple arthritis is inflammation of a joint, usually accompanied by pain, swelling, and frequent changes in structure. It might be noted that this differs from osteoarthritis and other forms of arthritis by the type of manifestation, and then there is a different spiritual route behind each of the types.

The spiritual root for simple arthritis involves bitterness against others. To help you understand, it seems when you have bitterness against yourself, it involves degeneration, but when you have bitterness against others, it involves swelling and inflammation. It is the swelling and inflammation that produces the deformity by Henry W. Wright.

Osteoarthritis is progressive cartilage degeneration in joints and vertebrae, and it usually does not involve inflammation. Cartilage is the other material between the vertebrae. Osteoarthritis is the result of self-bitterness and not forgiving oneself. It is holding a record of wrongs against yourself, and it can also involve an element of guilt to Henry W. Wright.

As I read through Henry W. Wright's book, I said well, I did it to myself. It's already there now. But God said. It's not too late. That is why I said *FORGIVE YOURSELF and decree and declare the Word of the Lord over your life.*

He is despised and rejected of men; a man of sorrows, and acquainted with grief: and we hid as it were our faces from him; he was despised, and we esteemed him not. Surely he hath borne our griefs and carried our sorrows: yet we did esteem him stricken, smitten of God, and afflicted. But he was wounded for our transgressions; he was bruised for our iniquities: the chastisement of our peace was upon him, and with his stripes, we are healed. Isaiah 53:3-5 KJV

After reading my Bible and Henry W. Wright's book, I went into prayer, repenting and renouncing the spiritual roots I believed about myself that affected my body. I had to come up against self, fear, anger, guilt, unforgiveness, and bitterness and believe in God for my healing. One thing I know is that forgiveness is key to me receiving what I need from God concerning my health; this can be like having a self-inflicted wound, causing a physical injury done to oneself by not forgiving yourself. Not forgiving myself left the door open for the enemy to have a legal right to come in and cause more injury to me. But the good news is that mentioned in 1 John 1:9 KJV *If we confess our sins, he is faithful and to forgive us our sins, and to cleanse us from all unrighteousness.*

One of the spiritual roots that I want to write about is bitterness because it goes hand in hand with unforgiveness. When you don't respond correctly when offended, bitterness is sure to spring up.

Looking diligently lest any man fail of the grace of God; lest any root of bitterness springing up trouble you, and thereby many be defiled. Hebrews 12:15 KJV

Bitterness means to be bitter, to cut, or to prick. The Bible says that this resentful, unforgiving attitude will cut and prick others as well. Bitterness is the result of not forgiving others. If you are bitter at someone, it means that you haven't truly forgiven that person. The enemy will make sure that things happen in your life to keep bitterness anchored in your soul so that you can't forgive. Bitterness has a purpose: to steal, kill, and destroy your life from the inside out.

Bitterness can affect your relationship with God, yourself, and others. The root of bitterness doesn't just affect you; it affects anyone around you, such as family or friends. It's a troubling root that's designed to prick you to where you can become bitter, too. My faith has not wavered, even knowing the reason behind the pain and the spiritual root. In fact, it went to another level of faith, believing in God for a miracle.

A few of my doctors said I didn't have to come back to them anymore because my tests came back normal, so I Praise God and give Him All the Glory! My friend and I have reconciled; she called me and asked me for forgiveness. The Power of Forgiveness can restore relationships and heal you in every area of your life.

Affirmation:

I choose to forgive; I choose to release the weight of resentment.

"In forgiveness, I choose to find freedom and peace.
In forgiveness, I choose to let go of the past and embrace the healing power of grace.
In forgiveness, I choose to move forward with a heart full of compassion, a renewed mind, and a right spirit.
In forgiveness, I choose to be empowered by the strength I found in forgiveness.
In forgiveness, I forgive me, Amen."

Apostle Tina M. Beatty

A postle Tina M. Beatty is the Founder and Senior Pastor of King of Glory International Ministries and Lion of Judah International Ministries in Charleston, West Virginia. She received her Doctorate of Divinity from St. Thomas Christian University. She has an Apostolic and Prophetic call upon her life, as well as a Deliverance Ministry. She is the wife of Ronald C. Beatty. They have four children, seven grandchildren, and many bonus grandchildren.

She has preached for churches and conferences nationally and internationally. She is the Founder and Visionary of I Lived To Tell It. As she continues to do the work of ministry she is not ashamed to tell her testimony of how she overcame, according to Revelation 12:11.

She is a Chaplain, Certified Life Coach/Trainer as well as an Entrepreneur having multiple streams of income, Nappy by Nature Salon, TMBeatty Ministries Inc., Strategic Life Coach Academy, I Lived To Tell It, LLC, Boutique and more.

Dr. Tina M. Beatty Books to purchase on Amazon:

Let's Write Together, Write Place, Write Time by Dr. Tina M. Beatty

Prayers that Open Heaven by Dr. Tina M. Beatty

My Sister Helped Me Heal Anthology Volume 1 Best Seller ~ Visionary Author ~ Dr. Chavon Anette. Chapter 17 A Mother's Love by Dr. Tina M. Beatty

I Survived the Storm Anthology Best Seller ~ Visionary Author ~ Dr. Paulette Harper. Chapter 6 ... It Happened Again by Dr. Tina M. Beatty

I Lived to Tell It Testimonial Anthology Best Seller and International Best Seller ~ Visionary Author ~ Dr. Tina M. Beatty. Chapter 10 ... Don't Say A Word

Don't say a word 12-day fasting journal ~ Dr. Tina M. Beatty

Groomed for His Glory Anthology ~ Visionary Author ~ Apostle Michelle Franklin. Section 1 ... Kingdom Women, Arise by Dr. Tina M. Beatty

Coming Soon: License to Carry Dr. Tina M. Beatty and The Chaplains Corner Anthology Visionary Author Michelle Franklin

Connect with Dr. Tina M. Beatty:

Facebook: Tina M. Beatty
Instagram: iam_tmbeatty
Website: ilivedtotellit.com
Email: apostletmbeattywva@yahoo.com

CHAPTER 2
Choosing Forgiveness: The Discovery and Redemption of a Father-Daughter Relationship

By Evangelist Lynn L. King

Forgiveness is a "Cold Piece" and can be the culprit of you doing what may seem ridiculous and strange, all while cutting you to the core and then healing you all at the same time! Forgiveness can send you on an emotional rollercoaster and then be one of the most impactful and best decisions you will ever make in your life! Let's journey down my path to forgiveness.

I need to go back to my childhood when I was informed that the man I had considered my father for the initial eight years of my life was no longer entitled to that role. Why? Because he was not my father. Although my mother and he were never married, they shared a lengthy history. It struck me as odd, however, that an unmarried pastor of a local church would be referred to as my father, but go figure!

I enjoyed having him in my life, from what I remember. I was even told that we had some of the same physical features. He and my mother were off and on; however, there came a time when he chose to move on and marry someone else. As a result of that decision, I remember being told that he was not my father and I could no longer address him as such. I was devastated! How could this be? Who would it be? If not him, then *who*?

In the fourth grade, walking home from school one bright and sunny day, a memory unfolded that I'll never forget. As I entered the house, my mother and a man sat on our big red couch. He seemed familiar, and indeed, I had seen him at church. Our home church had branched off from his, and we worshiped together for years. Little did I know that what would happen next could turn my world completely upside down.

The introduction went like this: "Hey, this is your father," followed by his name. There was no segue leading up to this life-altering news; no special outing or preparation. No "Sit down, let me talk to you about something." Nothing but a straightforward declaration: "This is your father."

We spoke briefly, and he gave me "a lil change," which was twenty dollars. I felt a momentary happiness, a childlike joy because I had a father again, and also because he considered twenty dollars as "lil change." What can I say? I was a nine-year-old in the fourth grade, thinking he was rich or something.

One might expect our relationship to blossom into a beautiful father-daughter redemption story, but it was far from that. I rarely saw him, mostly during joint church programs. I couldn't acknowledge him publicly because HE WAS MARRIED! No display of affection—every daughter's need. I just had to accept that I WAS ONE BIG SECRET, the elephant in the room, the skeleton in the closet.

My mother always waited for him after service; he would sneak away to talk to us and give us money. I looked forward to it, as financially, we struggled. Government assistance, Christmas boxes, cheese, and food stamps were our norm. When he came, I saw an opportunity for extra help, even paying bills. The dynamics of how I came into the equation puzzled me. Two church-going believers, both active leaders, had me without being married, and he was married to someone else. I knew I was a product of an affair, smart enough to understand, but it didn't make sense, and I was deeply hurt.

A bit of background: I was a girl who was taught right from wrong and understood it well. I tried my best to adhere to the foundational standards, but when I fell short, conviction and condemnation weighed heavily. I often confessed my shortcomings; though young, my perspective recognized the hypocrisy.

Initially, covert meetings occurred around the church involving him, my mom, and me. However, they evolved into private encounters between him and me, where we briefly talked, and I received money. Growing angry and resentful, I told my mother that his wife and I were the only victims, lacking a say in their selfish acts. I even threatened to reveal the truth, striking a nerve with my mother, who warned me against calling her. His wife knew me, not as my father's daughter, but as the little singing girl from church who grew up. They attended my high school graduation open house, providing a full luggage set for college. How awkward not being able to acknowledge our relationships during such a pivotal moment.

Off to college, I went, and the next few years mirrored the past. I'd meet him on breaks, still hidden from the world. Only a few people, to my knowledge, knew the truth—his church friend, some of my mother's close friends, and family. They all knew each other from church. Growing closer to God, reading His word, and worshiping Him, I became less understanding of the deception among believers who loved God. I couldn't comprehend why no one would come clean and tell the truth.

Resentment intensified, and my relationship with my father felt purely transactional. It served as a means to get extra dollars, meeting in an AA meeting parking lot, hardly ideal for relationship building. No one wanted to be honest for my sake as a daughter, her sake as a wife, or for the father/daughter relationship. It was a boiling "hot mess" in my eyes.

I received news that my father's wife had passed away. By then, an adult and a resident of W.V. where I attended college, my heart went out to her even more. For over twenty years, she lived unaware of her husband's daughter, whom she knew, and they never had children. Saddened by her passing, I became more upset. It felt unfair that I grew up impoverished while my well-off father lived nearby. Unfair that my mother and father determined the fate of a potentially good relationship. Now, she has passed on, and the truth remains unknown. It just wasn't fair. Sometimes, I think she must have known about me. Additionally, I wonder if she knew but chose not to acknowledge who I truly was.

After her death, my relationship with my father became more public. When we met, rare as it was, I was introduced as his daughter and he as my father. People were always shocked, their faces and smiles priceless. We communicated more, but a significant shift occurred when forgiveness took hold of me. Since then, my life has never been the same.

Having grown up, matured, and experienced life-altering events, I grasped the dynamics of repentance and forgiveness. Reflecting on my young adult years, I recognized that being an adult involves various levels and layers, with forgiveness being one of the most crucial. This paved the way for me to choose forgiveness not only for my father but also for my mother.

That's why I say forgiveness is a "Cold Piece!" It may feel like an overwhelming, difficult journey, but the greater reward awaits on the other side.

First, **I learned to accept forgiveness from God** (1 John 1:9 NIV). Despite feeling dealt an unfair hand, it wasn't my place to harbor unforgiveness against my father. His lack of an apology didn't excuse me from forgiving him. I lack the authority to judge, so even my father deserves forgiveness from God, as exemplified by Jesus on the cross: "Father, forgive them for they know not what they do."

Secondly, **I learned self-forgiveness is essential** (Hebrews 4:13 NIV). If God forgives us, we should too, as nothing remains uncovered under the blood of Jesus. He isn't surprised by anything we do on earth. Condemnation isn't of God, so avoid applying that pressure on yourself.

Thirdly, **I learned extending forgiveness to others is crucial** (Luke 23:34 NIV). Forgiving releases us from the weight of bondage, sickness, and disease, freeing us from a victim mentality. It helps us see people as God's creation with a soul needing saving, just like us.

Lastly, **I learned to accept requests for forgiveness.** (Matthew 6:14 NIV). I accepted my father's sincere apology, understanding that being vulnerable and having a pliable heart to accept apologies helps us mature in Christ Jesus. Holding grudges invites punishment from God, as He isn't pleased with it (refer to the scripture "Forgive us our debts as we forgive our debtors," Matthew 6:12).

I moved back to my hometown of Flint, MI, in my early thirties. During that time, I had candid conversations with my father, delving into his background, my family, and the connection between my mother and him. Being in his eighties, some details didn't matter as much.

Looking forward to being the daughter he never had and having the father I never had, we navigated these roles with humor. He walked me down the aisle, became a grandfather to our four children, and supported me when my mother passed away. Eleven months later, to the day of my mother's death, he also joined The Lord, but my heart found peace.

My decision to move back to Michigan was fully prompted by The Holy Spirit. After fasting and prayer, I realized I had to return as the Lord revealed my mission field was at home. Despite not understanding at first, within six years, I got married, became a mother, and lost both my parents. Activating the power of forgiveness was crucial. God, in His infinite wisdom, knew I needed to be home, fulfilling my mission upon my return. I reiterate that forgiveness is a "COLD PIECE," yet I'm grateful for the journey, a challenging yet transformative experience.

My Prayer For You:

Father God, in the name of Jesus, I pray for every person reading this testimony. I pray that it illuminates hope in their lives and that their hearts be softened and prompted to choose forgiveness at all costs.

Lord, I pray for that man and woman who are on the cusp of getting involved with one another for all of the wrong reasons. I pray that they have a Kairos moment that snaps them into the realization that there are consequences to EVERY decision, and most often, we don't control what that will be. In the event that they are now living with the fruit of their choices, my prayer is that they will trust you and know that whatever you allow to be revealed, you also have the power to heal! Increase their capacity to trust you.

Lord, remind them that the decisions that they make not only affect them but those closest to them and even generations to come. Give them the *mind* to be honest (about it), knowing that your Love covers all. Again, let them know that whatever you ALLOW to be revealed, you also have the POWER to heal.

I pray that the chokehold of pride and unforgiveness doesn't taint their lives and cause the vicious cycle of brokenness to run rampant through their family. The curse be broken now in Jesus' name.

I pray for children who are growing up not knowing who their father is or the truth about who THEY are. Protect their hearts, Oh God, and show them that you, Lord, are their Heavenly Father. Let it be known to them that you are a place of refuge where they can find Provision, Protection, Guidance, and Love. Lord, I know that you are able to remove the weight of unforgiveness, bitterness, and resentment from their lives as well. Lord, let them know that they have purpose and none are here by accident. Help them to look past the hurt and receive your forgiveness and that of others, knowing that in the end, you can turn every situation around for their good and for your Glory. In Jesus' name, I pray, Amen.

Evangelist Lynn L. King

Evangelist Lynn L. King is a native of Flint, MI, where she and her husband, Bruce King Jr. reside with their 5 children: Bri'Ana, Naomi, Nathan, David, Son-In-Love Malik, and their grandson Malik Jr. (MJ).

She accredits her ability in ministry to the strong foundation of leadership within her childhood church, Damascus Holy Life Baptist Church.

Over the span of her life, Lynn has sung in various gospel choirs, co-founded The Ladies Of My

Sister's Keeper, become a Worship Psalmist, and co-led the Young Adult and Youth Ministries of Refuge Temple Church of Flint, where she currently fellowships under the leadership of Pastor Matthew and Lady Abby Jackson.

In 2010, Lynn graduated from the Abundant Life Bible College with an associate degree in theology realizing that there is a "sermon" in her song.

In 2021, God called her to preach The Gospel of Jesus Christ and to create BOLD LIFE MINISTRIES for young ladies ages 14 to 22. BOLD LIFE MINISTRIES launched April 30th, 2022 and on June 5th, Lynn was anointed as an Evangelist alongside her husband as an Elder of Refuge Temple Church of Flint.

Lynn is a licensed cosmetologist of 25 years and co-owner of Synergy Beauty Studio in Flint, MI. Because of her own life's experiences she champions girls and the women that they become to live a BOLD life UNAPOLOGETICALLY! She can be found on Facebook and Instagram as Lynn L. King ~ That BOLD Coach.

~ "BE BOLD. BE BEAUTIFUL. BE YOU" ~

CHAPTER 3
Unraveling The Layers Of A Spiritual Onion
By Prophet Mattie Morgan

An "onion" is described as a round vegetable with a light brown skin. It has a thin or thicker layer on the inside, which produces a strong, sharp smell and taste. [1] The word "onion" comes from the Latin word 'union that' means unity or oneness. A union – like an onion, is dismantled or destroyed as it is gradually taken apart...layer by layer. [2] When I received the request to participate in this project, the spirit of the Lord showed me an onion and said, "Your deliverance will come in layers...just as you peel an onion." I heard this prior to saying "yes," so, after many attempts to abort this assignment, I relented to trusting the Creator to do some masterful work in my life.

Thelayers, each carrying a different degree and intensity of aromatic pain if you will. From childhood through adulthood, I wondered if there was an invisible mark on my head or a sign I wore that said, "Hurt me * pick on me, or my feelings don't matter!" In any situation, one must always look internally because you are *never* always innocent.

In early childhood, I remember in grade school, having helped pick up some currency a fellow student had thrown into the air and let fall onto the playground. When his willful act resulted in other students grabbing dollar bills, he didn't think it was such a good idea. He asked for help, so what I picked up was given to him [so I thought].

After returning to class after lunch, the door opened with an administrative staff, and I thought to be the kid I handed my fist full of money. Ironically, after repeatedly telling them I handed it to him, they realized I had given it to his twin brother. Although it was a seemingly minor incident, I did not understand all the implications behind the accusation. Unbeknownst to me, a layer was added to my onion.

At another time in my life, I did not understand nor have the intent to pursue the essence of integrity, honesty, or being dependable. However, with the many mishaps of growing up and trying to fit into my skin, it became important to me to do (to the best of my ability), what I committed to do. Whether I had a friend or not, I wanted to be loyal and trustworthy, so this whole internal montage of having a theme for my life evolved without me consciously being aware I needed to follow some type of path or direction.

There were a couple of incidents in high school where I cheated on a test; it was so evident to the teachers. In one scenario, a group of us decided to use some answers to a test, and someone passed them on to everyone in our little group. The failure occurred when they whispered to transfer the answers down one question. I changed everything I had done and, in so doing, failed the test, failed the class, and had to retake it again. All of my friends passed.

In another scenario, I was solely at fault! My instructor waited until class was over and asked me to stay back; she tore up my quiz, and what she said broke my spirit. She told me that I was a good student, and she was shocked that I would do something like cheat. Another layer added to my developing "onion."

Growing up, I heard repeated comments about my skin color/tone. It was something I could not change. I found myself getting comfort in and with the oddest things, including my dog. That dog was the greatest therapist around; he knew all my secrets, listened to all my stories, never said anything hurtful to me, and just let me talk and kind of figure things out.

He had such an amazing gift for just listening and would sometimes lick my tears. Those sessions taught me to talk to God, to sound out, and then listen for His answer. Sometimes, His answer(s) was not what I wanted to hear, but within each situation I found traumatic, I did not realize at the time that He was there for me to release these things I carried. I allowed these incidents to add a layer to my onion, even though my skill and ability to hear the Father was developing.

I had seven siblings, being the seventh of eight. My mother's first marriage resulted in my older sibling's father dying. She subsequently met and married my father. As a young girl, I put my older siblings on a pedestal. I idolized them; it was so funny when I was asked how many siblings I had because it took both hands for me to count. When we had an opportunity to get together, they would talk negatively about our mother, and over a period of time, I realized they did not care about us or our feelings.

I became numb to these repeated incidents; I was tired of being hurt by them because I could not change what happened or seemingly happened in the past. I was tired of them openly talking negatively about our mother. I realized no one does *everything* right, but I had enough understanding at a young age to realize that something was not right in these festering ramblings.

Over the past few years, some things have occurred that allow you to know God's Word is true. Whatever "seed" is sown *shall* produce a harvest! We are now seeing a door of forgiveness open. An older sibling verbalized her resentment that had grown to anger; the door has opened for repentance, deliverance, healing, and reconciliation for all of us. Love that had been held in reserve within me met her at the door.

God began melting my protective barrier of indifference, numbing, and resentment toward my siblings. Despite how it comes or how we respond to an issue, we are responsible for forgiving others *quickly* and not allowing what occurs to us to become a layer to our "onion." It is up to us as to whether we allow an offense to produce a harvest. Refusal to forgive or unforgiveness creates an offense or seed to develop roots in our lives.

    The enemy of our soul will go to great lengths to trap us or to use attractive bait to cause us to sin, diminish our zest for the Lord, or walk away from him completely. Look at and consider the depth of these scriptures:

Woe to the world because of the things that cause people to stumble! Such things must come, but woe to the person through whom they come!
- Matthew 18:7 [NIV]

Luke 17:1-4 [NIV] Jesus said to his disciples: "Things that cause people to stumble are bound to come, but woe to anyone through whom they come. 2 It would be better for them to be thrown into the sea with a millstone tied around their neck than to cause one of these little ones to stumble. 3 So watch yourselves. "If your brother or sister[a] sins against you, rebuke them; and if they repent, forgive them. 4 Even if they sin against you seven times in a day and seven times come back to you saying 'I repent,' you must forgive them."

There is an old trapping/hunting technique where a stick was used to prop up a box or container. Usually, a piece of meat or bait is tied to the stick that is particularly enticing to the prey being sought to trap; when the animal comes along, the aroma of the bait is secured, and by any means necessary, the animal is determined to get it from the stick. The animal will pull and tug, tug and pull, until the "skandalon/offense," the trigger of the trap, has firmly caught him! What if the enemy uses the "skandalon/the trigger/an offense/the bait/unforgiveness as a trap for us?

Scripture says *woe unto him who brings the offense*; but we who are offended have a responsibility as well. We are commanded to forgive not occasionally or on occasion, but this amazing scripture instructs us to do so 490 times – in one day!

Matthew 18:21-23 [NIV] - 21 Then Peter came to Jesus and asked, "Lord, how many times shall I forgive my brother or sister who sins against me? Up to seven times?" 22 Jesus answered, "I tell you, not seven times, but seventy-seven times. 23 "Therefore, the kingdom of heaven is like a king who wanted to settle accounts with his servants.

Although we have a bona fide reason to feel hurt and trespassed against, the Lord cautions us to be aware of the greater trap that has been laid out for us. A thief does not come to your house to meet with you, laying out a 90-day plan, or indicate by mail, "I am going to steal, kill, and/or destroy from you." He comes immediately with a trigger that is baited and set to lure us. As many layers as he can add to our "onion," the more indignant we can become and the more self-righteous we are about our stance.

Many times, we think we are okay. We think we are hiding the pain. We think we are able to "bite the bullet," so to speak, but in actuality, we limit ourselves naturally, spiritually, mentally, relationally, financially, and in so many other ways. What we hold inside and do not become delivered from often becomes a health issue.

In some instances, we are not cognizant of what is subliminally or unconsciously occurring in our lives. As the layers began to peel in *my* life, I found myself angered – just mad. Being a normally easy-going person and having anger boil from my innermost being. I knew there was an underlying problem.

I found myself repenting and asking God to take this anger from me and help me forgive people I did not even realize I held hostage. Wow!!! I then became a crybaby, and for about two weeks, I cried about so many things. I began remembering things I had not thought about since childhood.

As I mentioned at the onset, for me, it is layer by layer, step by step, day by day! Forgiveness is not for the weak; you must be honest with yourself and forgive yourself! There have been times I said, "Lord, slow down; I need to manage the removal of this layer. I need to understand this element you have exposed to me; I need to get through this before you take me through that!"

Since dealing with *me*, I have understood more clearly that truly being *His* servant comes differently for each of us. When you are ready to become vulnerable, when you are willing to lay it all down, and when you stand up to pride and tell him [pride] you are going to lift the layers, healing becomes your portion. At this point, it does not matter whether you are knowledgeable about what lies beneath the layers; trust the peel!

Jeremiah 31:3 [NIV] ~ The Lord appeared to us in the past, saying: "I have loved you with an everlasting love; I have drawn you with unfailing kindness.

We cannot control others, but the Lord tells us that offenses will come to root out, reveal, manifest, surface, or bring to the top what is in our hearts! I just kept things moving; surely "I" was not holding unforgiveness, I thought. Things were so suppressed it took the plan of the Lord to break away and lead me to a place of surrender. Although I did not think I was in this condition, the Spirit of the Lord knew it was time for the onion layers to peel. I am gaining strength and wholeness in allowing my spiritual "onion" to peel; how about you?

    I decree and declare that every heart that has not encountered spiritual forgiveness becomes flooded with the overwhelming love of the Heavenly Father. I decree that every subdued and suppressed emotion begins to bubble up and erupt from the crevices and deep places of the soul and be delivered, healed, and set free by the Power of God. I decree and declare a responding of new birth and a new zeal for the pursuit of the Lord and fulfillment of His will for each and everyone reading this anthology, in the name of the Lord.

Mattie Joyce Jordan Morgan

Mattie Joyce Jordan Morgan is the seventh of eight children. Her parents are Mattie Belle Cook Jordan and Stonewall Jordan of Red Jacket, WV. She graduated from high school at Magnolia High in Matewan, WV and attended college in Berea, Ky at Berea College where she obtained a bachelor of science degree in business administration. Although enjoying the administrative and accounting side of this field, there has always been an underlying love for writing.

Mattie heard the call of God as a fifth grader on the playground of her school, responding to the alter call the following Sunday with a subsequent baptism. She is blessed to serve Apostle-Dr. Tina M. Beatty at King of Glory International Ministries in the office of prophet and is honored to be the wife of her soulmate William [Bill] Morgan for twenty-nine years.

Mattie has fulfilled a contractual agreement with a private individual for over twelve years to write up to three messages annually. In the past she has assisted with the initial edit on a book project for Bishop William Compton; and has reviewed the initial writing for two audio albums for her mother, the late Mattie Belle Jordan. She has participated in a number of church plants; intricately involved in the birth of a dynamically growing children's ministries while in KY. In her leisure, she and Bill have restored cars, bred and raised purebred dogs, remodeled homes and completed specialty projects for ministers and close friends. Mattie loves the Lord and serving others.

CHAPTER 4
Inclined To Forgive
By April Battle

Our understanding of forgiving others has increased greatly. We understand the scripture, which tells us to forgive others, and we will be forgiven. When we show others grace for their wrongdoing toward us, our heavenly Father grants us the same level of grace for our own transgressions (Matthew 6:14-15 NIV). We have come to learn not to hold grudges against people for long because it takes up a great amount of our own time, energy, and effort when we do. Holding a grudge against someone interferes with our own peace of mind.

Many of us have experimented with testing the scripture on forgiving others and often feel a sense of peace and calm almost immediately towards others and within ourselves. Experiencing that peace has taught us the way to continuously have it is to work through any wrongdoing others may do to us and things we can control and deal with those accordingly. One might say that, as a result of this lesson, we have learned to chase after peace at all costs.

Although we have learned to forgive others, we have somehow never learned or even considered affording ourselves the same level of grace. The whole concept or thought of forgiving ourselves may seem foreign, as we often focus more on others than on ourselves. But today, let me share my personal journey of learning to give myself grace and to forgive myself.

Everyone assumes I am the nice one, the bright one, the positive one. The one who gets knocked down but gets back up stronger every time. She always bounces back better is what I've been told. I'm not sure where or how people came to that conclusion about me, but it just seems to stick. Over time, I've adopted it as my way of life.

April – the overcomer.

April – the one that's *always* okay.

April – the one that *will always* be okay. The one that overlooks how others may mistreat or disrespect her. The one that takes life's hits and uses them to grow. The one who just takes said hits, brushes them aside, and just keeps life moving with a smile on her face and a pleasant greeting and positive word for all. "Ever forward" is what I always say to myself and to others.

Yet, I still hurt. Yet, I still bear the scars of life. Yet, I give grace to others. Not always right away because I am human, after all. But in time, grace is always sufficient for others, just as the word tells us in

2 Corinthians 12:9 – But he said unto me, "My grace is sufficient for you, for my power is made perfect in weakness. Therefore, I will boast all the more gladly *about my weaknesses, so that Christ's power may rest on me."* New International Version. His grace is more than enough for me, so my grace is more than enough to give to others in spite of – yet, I still hurt. Yet, I still bear the scars of life.

As I stated, my grace and forgiveness of others are not always immediate, but eventually, I do forgive. The word tells us in *Matthew 6:14-15 – For if you forgive other people when they sin against you, your heavenly Father will also forgive you. But if you do not forgive others their sins, your Father will not forgive you sins. New International Version.* Many of us have come to understand that scripture so we may be forgiven by our Father. We may not necessarily associate ourselves with those people again, but we don't hold a long-term grudge against them. We forgive, learn, and let go.

The forgiveness I've given others has at times become a weight on me. Not that I carry the burden of the hurt or the scars, but as I age and mature in life, I find myself questioning and examining how I got myself into certain situations. How did I let certain things happen that led me to this place in life?

I often talk to myself, which some people have said is strange, but it helps me face my situations, come to conclusions, and develop resolutions. In examining myself, I've found my status in life, or my scars are not because of what others have done. It's all directly related to my own decisions. Decisions where I've allowed things to go in directions I knew weren't best for me, and as a result, I am left to deal with the consequences.

I've had to question myself – is it maybe me? Am I the reason I have these scars? Meaning, the way I respond to the things people may say or do to me. Is my response and allowing their words or actions to penetrate and infiltrate my very being the issue? I prayed and asked God to reveal the truth to me. The revelation was profound and unlike anything I could have ever imagined. The way to soothe and relieve the scars was not to just forgive, but to forgive myself.

This word was so new that I had zero understanding of what it meant. So, I walked away from it and just left it alone as if defying logic. It surely wasn't anything I'd heard taught or even spoken of. Now, looking at my scars and hurt took on a new point of view. But I still wrestled with some doubt on the concept and ability to forgive myself.

I questioned how do I even forgive myself. This concept of offering myself grace was not clear in the word, so it required me to do some in-depth studies. *Hebrews 12:1 states – "Therefore, since we are surrounded by such a great cloud of witnesses, let us throw off everything that hinders and the sin that so easily entangles. And let us run with perseverance the race marked out for us."* New International Version. The weight of holding on to my hurt and scars was burdening me to the point where I was stuck in life. As a result, I have learned to forgive myself.

It's okay, I made bad decisions and allowed others to interfere in my life and intercept my own sense of peace. I can admit the role I played, forgive it, and just let go. According to the word of God, those things no longer must entangle me. I can be free in my mind, which allows me to be free in my body, which allows me to be free in my spirit. I can tell April, it's okay. I can tell April that she is going to be okay and mean it with a better understanding. I can forgive April.

As stated in my bio, I am a licensed massage therapist and nail technician. I was studying to take an exam to obtain my nail tech instructor license, and one of the chapters in the textbook Milady Professional Education states - *<u>Practice personal forgiveness</u>. In order to develop a healthy set of values, we must be able to truly forgive ourselves for things that did not turn out the way we planned. If we can see our past failures as learning moments to improve, we will live a life with less regret. This will develop a higher sense of self-worth and empower us with more confidence (Milady's professional educator (4th ed). (2022.), Cengage, Practice personal forgiveness, p.45).*

I am not only learning to forgive but I am also permitting myself to forgive. There are several steps I follow regularly: 1) Be kind to myself; 2) Accept myself and my lack of perfection; 3) Care for myself first; 4) Be patient with myself; 5) Always seek out what I can learn in forgiving myself.

Imagine if we learn it's okay to forgive ourselves. If we learn it's okay to forgive ourselves, and a lot of the time, it's exactly what's needed. What if we learn and practice extending even more grace to ourselves than we extend to others? I believe once we do, we will experience a new sense of peace and calm deep within, and our lives will be better, and our relationships with others will be better.

If His grace is sufficient enough for us in all things, forgiving ourselves is included. Let's forgive.

Forgiveness Affirmation

Let's make the lessons and steps I've learned about forgiving ourselves as an affirmation in our lives so we can grow and experience the peace and freedom our Heavenly Father intended for us to live.

- I'll be kind to myself. We all make mistakes, and grace abounds.

- I will accept myself and my lack of perfection. I'm still a work in progress and will continue to grow and learn.

- I will care for myself first. I will forgive myself just as much or even quicker than I forgive others.

- I'll be patient with myself. I'm no longer reaching towards a lifetime goal when I still have a lifetime to live. I'll take it one day at a time.

- I will always seek out what I can learn in forgiving myself. Every opportunity is a lesson I can use along this journey.

April Battle

Being a native of Charleston, West Virginia, April is a Mountaineer by birth and at heart, and currently resides in Chesterfield County, Virginia, right outside of Richmond, Virginia. April is a mother of three (3) and a Nana to five (5) grandchildren.

She began her post graduate education a little later in life and obtained an Associate's of Applied Science in Massage Therapy from Columbus State Community College in 2007; a Bachelor of Science in Applied Management with a Minor in Small Business

Management in 2009 and a Master of Science in Marketing and Communication in 2012 Franklin University from Franklin University while living in Columbus, Ohio while raising her three (3) children as a single mother. Associates in Biblical Studies from Metropolitan College of Theology, Satellite Extension of North Carolina College of Theology in 2018.

April's love for the wellness and beauty industries combined has led her to open her own massage, spa, and wellness businesses, and to offer other services geared toward alternative forms of wellness. With her 15+ years of experience as licensed massage therapist and a nail technician, April is currently working toward opening a school which offers education in massage therapy, nail technology, as well as other forms of wellness to professionals and the general public to learn and advance their lives. She is a national speaker in the massage therapy field and as a perpetual learner, April stays up to date on changes to laws, techniques, and trends in her particular industries.

Her favorite part of the industry is teaching and seeing the moment and joy when a student "just get's it". When a student understands the concepts and how it can be applied to their daily lives and long-term success.

CHAPTER 5
How Can You Be a Daughter to a Stranger?

By Marian B. Jones-Allen

Our Heavenly Father tells us that, "For if you forgive men when they sin against you your heavenly Father will also forgive you" - Matthew 6:14 NIV

An excerpt, from the *From, La Christina* counselling.com biblical definition of forgiveness is the act of pardoning an offender. In this article, they provide eight steps to achieve forgiveness:

1. Acknowledge the pain.
2. Think through things.
3. Imagine being on the other side.
4. Remember God's forgiveness.
5. Reflect on our Biblical command [to forgive].
6. Let go of the hurt.

7. Continue to forgive.
8. Pray for the person who hurt you.

I am authoring this chapter from the perspective of my eleven-year-old self.
Growing up in a family of nine – mom, dad, and seven children was dynamic, loud, and, most of all, loving. My mother, a woman of small stature, loved the chaos of each day because, as an only child, she longed for other siblings to share in her youth. My dad, a large and powerful man, demanded respect from his own and all the neighbor's children as well. He ruled his household with an iron fist but doted on me, his first girlchild, after siring three boys. He would take me everywhere to show me off. I felt so special as the baby-sister or "Ba-Sis" for short. After my birth came another boy and then two girls.

Puberty interceded in my life, and at eleven years old, my menstrual cycle began. That memorable day found me at home from school and, sitting in the living room, I was confused when I saw my dad coming downstairs with an army green footlocker and duffel bag. He explained that he was taking his clothes to the cleaners. Even as an eleven-year-old, I knew that his statement did not make much sense. That was the last time that I saw or heard from him.

From that day on, our family's life changed dramatically. Our stay-at-home mom had to find a job to support her family even though she did not have a high school education. Our grandparents had to move in with us to help pay the bills, we had to go on welfare, and for the first time, we realized we were poor.

My mom found work as a domestic, and because the adults had to work to support our growing family, I was called upon to fill the role of pseudo-mother. I cooked, helped my siblings with their homework, ensured that the house was kept in order, laundered and ironed our clothes, and went grocery shopping with my mom once a month. Ripping the food stamps from the multi-colored booklets signaled to everyone that you were "dirt poor."

It is six o'clock in the morning, and my mom wakes me up. We must go to the Rescue Mission and sometimes to the Saint Vincent de Paul second-hand stores to get the "best" shoes and clothes to fit our growing family before the other shoppers arrive. Once a month, this early rising was so we could get to the laundry to get the best washers (all in a row) and the hottest dryers.

Meanwhile, I excelled at school. I always recall my dad telling me that I was very smart. I absolutely loved to read and would escape into the books and old movies on our black-and-white television that I enjoyed on the weekends. This was my life.

The year before my dad left his family, I watched as my mother fought for her life because of uterine cancer. The radio-active pack that the doctors placed in her womb meant that every day, my grandmother and I had to administer the twenty-one bottles of prescription medications that lined her dresser. I watched as she lost her hair, weight, and sweet voice as the disease and cure ravaged her petite body. She later told me that she had turned her face to the wall and pleaded with God, as Hezekiah did in Isaiah 38:2-6, to let her live to see her two-year-old baby girl graduate from high school. With God's blessing, she not only lived to see her baby girl graduate from high school but attend college, get married, and become a mother herself.

To her credit, my mother never spoke about our dad's leaving nor the circumstances that led to it. We did not ask about it because a child had to stay in a child's place when it came to grownup issues. She went about caring for her household. As for me, I began to resent the man that was our father. I could not enjoy the things other young ladies could because my mom and grandmother worked to put food on our table, clothes on our backs, shoes on our feet, and a roof over our heads. There were times that the gas and/or electricity was turned off, and we had to borrow food from our neighbors or get food on credit from the corner grocery store. But each Christmas, each child had a new toy, a new coat, shoes, and outfit, and a shoebox filled with a tangerine, peppermint stick, and mixed nuts.

But, life went on for our family. I continued to excel in school and filled the role of pseudo-mom at our house. One day, I was called to the high school counselor's office. I wondered what Ms. Boone wanted from me. I was never in trouble. When I entered her office, she told me that she had reviewed my grades and wondered why I was not in college prep classes. I admitted our family circumstances and told her that I would graduate and get a job as a secretary to help my family. She told me I would help my family more by attending college and getting a job that would pay more.

The next semester, I found myself enrolled in college prep courses. The coursework was not difficult, and I continued to excel. With the help of Ms. Boone and Mr. Singleton, a community activist, at the age of sixteen, I was granted a full academic scholarship to Mr. Singleton's alma mater and graduated Magna Cum Laude from Lincoln University in Pennsylvania.

My spiritual journey, however, continued to grow as I saw the circumstances of my life beginning to change. After college, I married and conceived my beautiful and accomplished daughter, Lauren, and because all things do not always work out as we think they will, I found myself divorced, away from my childhood home, and without any close friends in Washington, DC, my new home. But one day, while taking a quiet moment to have lunch, a man introduced himself.

He said, "You look like you are having problems. Let me tell you about my life."

James Allen told me about his life and his many struggles from high school through his own divorce circumstances (but that's another story). From that point on, we became close friends. So, I asked him if I could rent a room from him so that my daughter and I could have a place to stay until I found a place for the two of us. He reluctantly agreed. With his coaching, after a few months, I became a homeowner.

The next time I heard from my father, I was twenty-eight years old after a visit to his half-brother, Arthur, who lived in California. James encouraged me to try and talk with my father and make amends, something that he never had an opportunity to do. I did not see and/or speak to my dad during this visit, even though my aunt told me that my dad could see me from their backyard.

The phone rang early in the morning. You know those calls in the middle of the night that wake you up, and you know that something is wrong. It was my dad. I remembered his voice and will never forget what he said to me.

He asked, "What the hell do you want? I don't have anything for you."

I could not believe the arrogance. No hello. No, how are you doing? No, I'm sorry it took so long for me to contact you. Nothing.

As he was giving me the business, my spirit harkened back to how my mother had not focused on his absence, and the Holy Spirit said, *"Bless them that curse you, and pray for them which despitefully use you. Be ye therefore merciful as your father also is merciful. Judge not, and ye shall not be judged; condemn not, and ye shall not be condemned; forgive not, and ye shall not be forgiven"* (Luke 6:28; 36-37 KJV). If my mother could forgive him, so could I.

I asked him not to call me back, given how he chose to speak to me after eighteen years. I was so shaken. I could not believe it. I could not go back to sleep, but my resentment of everything I thought I had missed quickly ebbed away!

Afterward, I fell into a peaceful sleep. I felt lighter, but most of all, I knew my spiritual life had grown and would continue to grow within me. As expressed, "Now unto Him that is able to do exceedingly abundantly above all we ask or think, according to the power that worketh in us" (Ephesians 3:20 KJV).

Epilogue

Life continued and the friendship with James Allen blossomed into a proposal of marriage. The deciding factor of my "yes" was his love for God. After twenty-six years of marriage, the Lord called him home. Shortly thereafter, I received a call from my stepsister. She told me our dad had mentioned my name and wanted to speak to me. She asked if she could provide him with my phone number. I gave her permission. Two days later, in October 2023, at the age of sixty-eight, I again heard from my dad.

The ninety-one-year-old told me he wanted to "tell me his side of the story" of why he felt he had to walk away from seven children and another daughter that he had sired while still living in our hometown while married to my mother.

His "side of the story" began by referring to my grandmother and mother as fallen women and other nasty terms. I rebuked him and told him I would not continue this conversation if he referred to the two women who held our family together when he left. He talked for more than an hour as I listened, only interrupting when he again described my mother, who fought cancer and provided for our family, as a fallen woman and the like.

Throughout the conversation, I repeatedly asked him why he had not stayed connected with his eight children. After more excuses and what seemed to me more blaming others, he finally said, "I did not stay in contact because I knew if I did so, I would have come back, and I told your mother that if I left, I would never return."

I asked him what that had to do with staying in touch with his children, "Not a birthday card, an acknowledgment of graduating from high school or college, or just to say hello."

His final response was that he saw that I did not understand, and he was not looking for forgiveness from anyone, not even me, because he had to live his life, and he did just that! He just wanted me to hear his side of the story. After telling me the exact number of minutes down to the number of seconds we had been on the phone, he provided a return phone number to contact him. We said goodbye. When I tried to call him back to verify if the phone number he had given me was correct, the call was to a wrong number. Since my phone captured the number that I last received, I called him back. He said he knew he had provided the wrong number.

Unforgiveness is a heavy burden, but Jesus said that we should come to Him because His burden is light. You are forgiven because our God first forgave us. My burden of forgiveness has been lifted, but the question remains, how can you be a daughter to a stranger?

– An abandoned daughter

Affirmation

"Be anxious for nothing but in everything by prayer and supplication, with Thanksgiving, make your requests be made known unto God. And the peace of God which surpasses all understanding will guard your hearts and minds through Christ Jesus"
- Philippians 4:6-7 KJV.

I recite this every day to begin my quiet time with the Lord. It settles me as I move through the day and strengthens me for whatever He has coming my way.

Marian B. Jones-Allen

Marian B. Jones-Allen was born in Trenton, NJ and currently resides in Washington, DC. In 1972, at the age of 16, she graduated from Trenton Central High School. Upon graduating, she attended Lincoln University in Pennsylvania, receiving a Magna Cum Laude Bachelor of Arts degree in Sociology in 1976. At the age of 12, she focused on building a closer relationship with God, which was the start of her faith journey and continues to define her life today. She is the eldest daughter of seven siblings born to the late Bessie M. Jones. Upon the diagnosis of her mother's inoperable uterine cancer, Marion drew closer to the Lord for guidance and acceptance of such horrible news. During this challenging time, while struggling to be brave in support of her mother, she endured more heartbreak from her father, William A. Jones, who walked away from the family with no explanation. Life had been very linear at this time as she moved to Washington, DC in pursuit of obtaining a master's degree from the American University. She detoured from her studies into full-time employment with a utility company and later gave birth to her beautiful daughter, Lauren S. Haynie. She dedicated 32 years of employment at the utility company thriving in various roles, culminating her career as a Human Resource Business Partner. While employed, she met and was blessed to marry her late husband James M. Allen Sr. She is now happily enjoying retirement!

CHAPTER 6
Why Me, God?
By Prophet Carlotta Lynch

"Why me, God?" That was the question I'd asked God over and over. Years ago, I changed my life by accepting Jesus Christ as my Savior. In Christian settings, I am recognized as a woman of God. I thought I was doing what I felt was right to do. But the real truth is that "There is a way that seems right to a man, but its end is death" (Proverbs 16:5, New King James Version).

So, why did I ask the question, "Why me, God?" Well, I could also ask the question, "Why does this keep happening in my life?" What is the "this?" The "this" is that I consistently involve myself in ungodly relationships. Then I asked myself, "Why does this keep happening?"

I also kept asking myself, "How does a woman of God find herself in a cycle of continuous hurt, emotional turmoil, and, yes, even a kind of spiritual suicide? I knew that I had been made dead to sin when I accepted Jesus Christ. I thought I had died to my old life. I thought I had died to my will, ego, and ambition. I tried to humble myself, stay low, and not walk in pride. I proclaimed, "Christ is Lord, and I submit." I said this all so passionately - so I thought. But like many who may read this chapter, I had mastered the art of performing instead of practicing how to live in Christ and actually following the leading of the Holy Spirit.

"Why me, God?" I didn't seek to be in these ungodly relationships. I didn't seek to choose them over you(God). So,"Why Me God? Every time I found myself asking God this question, I now know I was in a state of guilt, shame, and condemnation. Feelings, of course, not of God! But I had begun to hate myself. I would fast, pray, and seek God's face, but I didn't understand why I was so weak. I would want to give up; I would perform for a while but then end right back in another ungodly relationship. This way of life and state of mind was certainly not the place of righteousness, peace, and joy that Jesus intended for me.

What is an ungodly relationship? Simply put, it is a relationship in which God is not present. I wondered why, as a believer in Christ, I would love and become involved with someone who doesn't love God as I do. They say they do but there is no fruit of the spirit. The fruit of goodness, righteousness, and truth were not exemplified (Ephesians 5:9 NKJV). There was no good coming from these relationships and plenty of lies.

"Why me, God?" What is wrong with me? I had engaged too many times with unclean spirits, and I felt filthy. How does a woman of God get to such a place in her behavior and within herself? I had engaged in these ungodly relationships, and I became corrupted and contaminated somewhere amid the company I entertained. "Evil company corrupts good habits" (1 Corinthians 15:33 NKJV).

I had a strong desire for what I call the "Bad Boy Syndrome." (That's another chapter for a future book.) Unconsciously, I was singing the movie song, "Bad Boy, Bad Boy, whatcha gonna do. Whatcha gonna do when come for you?" I thought I could change that tune to "Good Boy! Good Boy!" I thought I could save them. I considered myself mentoring them. I thought I was being a light to them in a dark world. I thought I was showing them what a woman of God looks like. I was deceiving myself. So, after the fourth Bad Boy – when I ended up in pain and suffering and almost gave up my spiritual walk again, I asked the same question again: "God, Why Me?"

Holy Spirit spoke to my inner being and said, "It's you."

I said, "ME!!" Then I didn't hear anything. There was silence.

There was silence from God for the next two months. I didn't hear anything in the spirit, but it was getting noisy in the natural. Rumors were being spread about me that shook my being. I was messing up at work. I was at church but not there mentally. And in the midst of my seeking God for clarity, I did hear, "Run for life and run <u>for</u> your life!"

The last two bad boys had declared war on me - a war where I knew I would be a causality. I knew if I stayed in the city I was in, something really bad would happen. I asked Daddy God to please provide a way of escape, and He did.

When I got to my new destination it was like the fog had cleared up. I could see so clearly. There were people there that God sent to love on me. But one in particular, a well-known author and teacher, just happened to be staying at the hotel I was running. I was in shock when I saw her. I couldn't believe the woman of God whose many books I had read and who I listened to on TV was standing in my hotel lobby. Well, me being me, I approached her and welcomed her to the hotel, and started talking to her like I had known her for years. Her daughter even said, "Mom, have you met her before?"

I thought that was funny. They asked me to come to church and offered to let me ride with them.

I didn't know that the church was about an hour away in the middle of nowhere. It seemed like it took forever to get there. I didn't know why I was so fidgety. This occurrence was like a dream come true. I felt I was in the presence of greatness. Knowing that she and her daughter were both speaking at the church, I tried to remain quiet and let them be. But both wouldn't let me be! The next thing I know, out the mouth of this great woman of God, I heard, "YOU! It's YOU!" I couldn't even speak.

She said, "Honey, you said you read my books and have heard me speak several times. So, you know my testimony. It's all about forgiveness. Forgive yourself!"

I was in shock. You would have thought she was talking in a foreign language. I just sat there confused. We all know where that came from. Because we know *"God is not the author of confusion but peace"* (1 Corinthians 14:33), that Word was for me. I thought we would never get to the church! We finally arrived, and she asked me, "Are you okay?"

I said, "Yes," but I wasn't really.

Again, my question, "God, Why Me? What is this? What is still going on?" I thought I had forgiven all these "bad boys" for everything they did to me. I experienced betrayal, domestic violence, and abandonment. But I had to realize that I played a part in whatever had happened to me. In coming to this reality, I knew I had to forgive them. Even though I had hurt, pain, suffering, and anger, I forgave them. So, what's this idea about forgiving myself? I was so insistent about asking, "God, Why Me?" when forgiveness for myself was part of my healing process the whole time. I needed to end my victim mentality in order to truly to move forward.

I pondered all of this throughout the whole service that evening. I still didn't understand. As a "victim," I think I didn't really want to understand. But when I got home, I sat on the couch and just started crying. Going through my head were thoughts of failure. I had failed to turn "bad boys" into "good boys" or save them. I had failed by not choosing and not dating the "right" men. I felt I had failed my family and friends. I felt I had failed my boss and employees. I began to think that I had failed the people I mentored and who had to endure all these rumors about me. Most of all, I felt that I had failed God!! I just failed! I hated myself for not being where I should be. After all, I should have known better, right?

Well, after all the praying, fasting, "churching," and reading the Bible, I felt that I had failed myself. But really, I was holding myself in unforgiveness. God did not consider me a failure!

Forgiveness has many definitions, but I want to share the following according to www.apa.com: *"Forgiveness is not merely accepting what happened or ceasing to be angry. It involves a voluntary transformation of your feelings, attitudes, and behavior so that you are no longer dominated by resentment and can express compassion, generosity, or even like the person who wronged you"* Even if that person is you! Powerful! I had wronged myself. I walked myself through deliverance that night. I repented, asked God to forgive me, and then forgave myself!

The next day at work, I saw the woman of God. She looked at me and said, "Freedom looks good on you. Now stay Free. Do whatever it takes to keep yourself free."

So, my fellow readers, I did just that. I started living my blessed life in Jesus. I had a new city, a new job, a new place, and a new church and new Pastor. I made choices in dating (lol) and began to enjoy just having fun. I began living like the daughter Daddy God called me to be. I was walking in the power of forgiveness. No more, ""Why me, God?" " but more of the truth of John 8:38, which says the following:

"Therefore if the Son makes you free, you shall be free indeed" (NKJV).

As I have shared a piece of my testimony, there is way more to the story. But I truly hope those who have found themselves in a similar situation and/or are asking the question, "Why me, God?" will have the time to start the process of healing by first forgiving themselves. It will be one of the best choices you can make – only after accepting Jesus Christ as your Lord and Savior. In writing this chapter, I desire that someone would not continue in a cycle that could be death to your spirit and soul. Allow grace and mercy and the power of forgiving yourself to have their way in your life.

I want to invite you to speak this affirmation out loud. I do this daily.

I am acceptable! I am valuable!
I am capable! I am forgivable!
How high will I let God take me?
I'm going all the way!

(JetLife Affirmation: Written by Carlotta Lynch Inspired by Peter 2:9)

My final words: no more, "Why me, God?" I am free indeed! I am forgiven!"

Carlotta Lynch

Carlotta Lynch, A prophetic voice that uplifts, encourages, and activates. She is a dynamic Inspirational Speaker with strong manifestations of deliverance. Her Marketplace anointing has allowed her to start up JetLife Consulting where she travels the world using her experience in Hospitality Management and Ministry Gifts to help businesses be more profitable and most of all impact people's lives for God's Glory.

Her mission statement says it all. "How high will let God take you? I'm going all the way!"

CHAPTER 7
The Rebirthing ~ Behold, I Am Doing Something New

By Apostle Michelle Franklin

Behold, I am doing a new thing; now it springs forth, do you not perceive it?
I will make a way in the wilderness
and rivers in the desert.
Isaiah 43:19

There have been a lot of ups and downs in my life. It seems like I've been on a never-ending roller coaster. I've cried tears of joy and tears of sadness. Through it all, the Lord has been right by my side. Leading me, guiding me, and encouraging me to keep pressing through. He knew where He was taking me, so I had to just follow. It wasn't until I let go and allowed Him to lead me in every area of my life.

I had to learn how to trust Him with all of my heart. Now, I feel like I'm living my best life. This is my moment. I tell myself that every day and anytime, things appear to be taking a turn. My Heavenly Father rebirthed me. He changed me, and I'm forever grateful. I was starting to get depressed. I felt like the world was against me, and nobody cared. In every direction, there was someone waiting to suck me dry and leave me hanging in the end as if I didn't matter.

I felt like I had no one to talk to about it without their judgment and opinions. As humans, we think we can fix everything, but the good Lord didn't give us the power to fix everything or everyone. Letting go was hard but worth it.

I feel like I'm living a dream that I never dreamed of. The Bible says that He will give you the desires of your heart. (Psalm 37:4) *Delight yourself in the LORD, and he will give you the desires of your heart.* When I let go and gave my problems to Him, He gave me His desires, which are so much better than I could have ever dreamed of.

I can remember being asked to preach at my cousin's home-going service at the beginning of August 2023. There were people from all over coming to pay their respects. During the repast, I ran into an old friend who asked me where I was living. I told him I was still living in the south suburbs. He yells, "Oh, so you're still with your parents?" I felt so embarrassed.

At 44 years old, I was still living with my parents. It didn't matter how I ended up back there; the point is I was there, and people had begun to wonder how I was preaching yet, still having money issues, and living with my parents.

When I got into the car, I cried. I said, "Lord, I make you look bad. I'm embarrassed, and I'm tired."

I didn't wait to see if the Lord would say anything back to me because I didn't want to be comforted by Him telling me that one day things would get better. I had already been waiting for years, so I didn't need another *one day*. I needed something *now*! So, I went home and went straight to bed. The next morning, as I was driving to work, I started praising God.

I said, "Lord, this year isn't over yet. I know You, and I know You can change things suddenly. You can change my situation before the end of the year."

Right after I said that, I received a call about a job interview of a lifetime; three days later, I was hired, and the job required me to move and offered me a salary three times the amount I have ever made in my life. After crying out to the Lord in less than a week, my situation shifted. I was overwhelmed with joy. I was speechless, and I knew that all my Heavenly Father wanted was for me to put Him in remembrance of His word and ask Him to do it. Sometimes, we get beside ourselves and think that God is mandated to move when we want Him without seeking Him.

This is the season He births new things around me and within me. I realized that the process was worth it. My hard work and my faith in my Heavenly Father had paid off. Not that I only wanted His deeds. I just wanted to make Him proud and glorify Him in every way possible, even in my deeds.

When people see the goodness of the Lord, it changes them. (Romans 2:4) *Or despisest thou the riches of His goodness and forbearance and long-suffering, not knowing that the goodness of God leadeth thee to repentance?* This is why it's important for His goodness to be seen in our lives.

I've learned that our lives are full of testimonies. Every day we rise, it produces a new testimony within – A story that glorifies our wonderful Heavenly Father. People are delivered because we are telling His story of how He rebirths us. I want to encourage you by letting you know that He knows, He hears your heart, and He's waiting on you to put Him in remembrance of His word. God bless!

Apostle Michelle Franklin

Michelle Franklin has been trained by Pastor John Maxwell's Team, Apostle Mark Walker Jr, Prophet John Veal, and Pastor Anthony Tiller, and sits under the leadership of Apostle Tina M. Beatty & Apostle JaMarr & Prophet Christina Gearlds. She's served in ministry for over 20 years.

    Ms. Franklin has demonstrated effective organizational and communication skills throughout her years in Ministry and Marketplace. She has exceptional leadership skills management skills and is considered a solution-oriented leader. She prides herself on building strong relational and interpersonal skills within teams and believes in professionalism and ministerial ethics to the highest degree.

Michelle Franklin holds a Minister License from IIFBC and King of Glory located in West Virginia, a License Board certified Biblical Therapist, Certified Christian Counselor, and serves as a Professional Clinical Hospice Chaplain, where she works within the hospital, assisted living, nursing home, and home health settings. Ms, Franklin holds a certification in community health work, a bachelor's degree in theology, and a master's degree in divinity.

She served as Executive Pastor at Faith on Fire Worship Center located in Dolton IL for 5 years, served as a Lead Prophet under Kingdom Empowerment Fellowship located in Dalton, Ga for 8 years, served as the Apostolic leader to The Apostolic World-Wide Mission Church in Kenya for 4 years, and is the Overseer of Life & Truth House of Worship, where she covers a variety of ministry gifts. She's trained National & International leaders in her years of serving and is a spiritual counselor and midwife to many. She is an affirmed Prophet/Apostle graced with an Apostolic mantle to build God's people by teaching them how to execute Kingdom principles in Ministry and the Marketplace.

She's knowledgeable in Psychology, Mental Health and skilled in grief recovery. Some of her experiences includes counseling, coaching, speaking, teaching, and training. She's a published Author of 22 books and has helped a diverse group of men and women across the United States become Authors. She believes in accountability and submits to an entire board of trusted, dependable, and integral Leaders. Ms. Franklin has experience as a keynote Speaker, and she's been done a variety of panel round-table discussions, breakout sessions and well equipped to serve in any capacity.

CHAPTER 8
Get Freed To Set Free
By Minister Samantha Stanley

I have been very blessed to experience the mercy and grace of the Hand of God from an early age. Of course, hindsight is 20/20, and I had seen, as I mature, that mercy and grace were especially covering me before I was truly saved when I could not keep myself.

However, being blessed never means that we will not endure trials, tribulations, and hardships. Usually, it means the complete opposite. Unfortunately, often, that means people will come against you, sometimes because of the anointing on your life, sometimes because they have not truly known the Lord and are operating by the agenda of this world, among other reasons.

Growing up, I had so many reasons to be mad at people. I could have easily been mad at my father, a binge alcoholic, who would verbally assault me when the beer took over. I could be mad at men who would ogle and molest me and try to manipulate me in what they supposed was my ignorance, albeit I paid careful attention to everything. I could be mad at the line of people who bullied me throughout school, to the point of my first suicide plan at age 12, the second (and last in Jesus' Name) being at age 25.

However, I now know it was necessary to perfect my testimony and ministry. I also know God had to permit the enemy to afflict as he requested permission to afflict Job, as shown in Job 2:3 KJV, *And the LORD said unto Satan, Hast thou considered my servant Job, that there is none like him in the earth, a perfect and an upright man, one that feareth God, and escheweth evil? and still, he holdeth fast his integrity, although thou movest me against him, to destroy him without cause.*

It was not easy when I ultimately gave my life to Christ wholeheartedly. I was afflicted in my mind with anger, frustration, toxic relationships, and hard-heartedness, as well as in my body with epileptic seizures, migraines, (natural) heart issues, and the list goes on.

However, as I studied the Word, I found conviction and consolation in the Parable of the Unforgiving Servant, where Jesus teaches that the man, when he was forgiven of such a large debt, was still unwilling to forgive his fellow servant of a very minute debt. As shown in Matthew 18:32-35 KJV, *Then his Lord, after that he had called him, said unto him, O thou wicked servant, I forgave thee all that debt, because thou desiredst me: shouldest not thou also have had compassion on thy fellowservant, even as I had pity on thee? And his Lord was wroth, and delivered him to the tormentors, till he should pay all that was due unto him. So likewise shall my heavenly Father do also unto you, if ye from your hearts forgive not every one his brother their trespasses.*

It came to my conscious that for all the evil I had been forgiven by my Lord, why should I not forgive others? Why should I not forgive all the men who had tried to overtake me? Why should I not forgive the ones who depressed me to the point of self-loathing? Why should I not forgive myself?

Notwithstanding all the issues I had dealt with through others' hands, I had committed most of the abuse. I was the one who berated myself, the one who told me I was not worthy, that I could not muster the integrity and boldness to operate in the call of God on my life. I must have never been called to preach; I must have never been called to prophesy or intercede. Even if I had been called to do all these things, I did not have the background or education for it. I did not know all the protocols the Church said I had to master.

The Word states in Amos 7:14-15 KJV, *Then answered Amos, and said to Amaziah, I was no prophet, neither was I a prophet's son; but I was an herdman, and a gatherer of sycomore fruit: and the LORD took me as I followed the flock, and the LORD said unto me, Go, prophesy unto my people Israel.* My favorite aspect of that scripture is Amos' emphasis on the fact that he (past tense) WAS not all of those things. However, as he obeyed, listened, and supped with the Lord, he heard his call and wholeheartedly obeyed. When I realized I was worthy, I was also worthy of complete forgiveness.

The moment I realized self-forgiveness was the moment I received freedom. It was the moment I received the full healing and peace that the Savior promised. It was the moment I realized that I could forgive all those who had, currently are, and would in the future, wrong me.

Many are troubled over trivial things; however, these were the hardest parts; these were the things that I especially had to seek the Lord for. I never ever desired that a trivial, non-foundational blip would become capable of destroying not just natural relationships but would deter someone so strongly that they would disavow Christ and surrender their relationship with Him.

Through all these trials and tribulations, I realized that if I could not get free from the shackles that had bound me all this time, how was I meant to set others free from the warfare that so oppressed them? I could not, in any way. I absolutely had to get free to set others free. The blind cannot try to lead the blind. If you are truly going to set others free from the bonds of sin and shame, don't you have to be free yourself? Don't you have to be freed before you can bail others out? Absolutely! I, of course, know that a singular human being in our own power could never set anyone free. Our flesh and the ties of sin that bind keep us from doing that. However, when we allow ourselves to be poured out and become empty vessels of the Lord, that is when we have potential. When we allow the Potter to mold us and shape us in our image while eliminating the issues, problems, faults, and general stumbling blocks, that is when we can expect to be made fit for the Master's use.

One of my absolutely favorite Bible stories is that of the Levite's Concubine, which recalls how this particular woman was attacked, molested, and ultimately died at the hands of her wicked abusers. Judges 19:26-27 (KJV) recounts, *Then came the woman in the dawning of the day, and fell down at the door of the man's house where her Lord was, till it was light. And her Lord rose up in the morning, and opened the doors of the house, and went out to go his way: and, behold, the woman his concubine was fallen down at the door of the house, and her hands were upon the threshold.* No matter what we let go of, whether it is unforgiveness, hatred, ought, or whatever, the one thing we must never give up on is the Lord God and His house. The Lord used the woman's demise to not only avenge her but the entire Nation of Israel.

In the same way, once we take our hands off of our problems and place our hands in the Master's hands, He is able to use us. He will use the area we have been hurt within and make that our biggest ministry. If you are an addict, God can use you in recovery. If church folks have hurt you, God can use you in reconciliation. For those who have had health issues, God will use your hands for healing. Those who have been battered, God will use you to help those who have been battered in the same way. No matter what, never ever, ever, let go of God's hand, and He will lead you into the call you have had on your life since before Creation.

Prayer

Father,

We thank you and praise you for all that you do. We give you glory and honor for everything you have brought us out of and everything you are currently bringing us out of. We thank you that everything is being done for our good and for your Glory.

    We pray you would soften our hearts, mold us, and shape us to your will and for your use. We pray you will help us to understand your will, no matter where it takes place or what it entails. Your word says the unforgiving cannot be forgiven, so, Lord God, we ask you to help us forgive. We ask your help to forgive our trespassers as they trespass against us, even when that trespasser is ourselves.

    We pray that you will give grace for the calling you have for us. Use us as a vessel to win others to you. We thank You for promising us we would not receive more than we can bear without You giving us a way of escape. We give you all glory, honor, and praise on Earth as it is in Heaven. All these things according to your will we ask.

In Jesus Name,
Amen

Samantha Stanley

Samantha Nicole Stanley was born in Charleston, West Virginia, and raised in Cabin Creek, West Virginia, the daughter of Brenda and the late Gary Stanley. She believed in the Lord at a young age and rededicated her life in 2014. She is a graduate of Riverside High School, West Virginia University Institute of Technology, and Ben Franklin Career Center.

She began attending church in 2015 at Living Waters Family Worship Center (Now New Mercies

Ministries) under Pastors Terrance and Angela Hamm. She currently attends and serves as Youth Minister at Jordan Outreach Center (formerly Gallagher Baptist Church) under Apostle Robin Davis.

She was ordained as a minister in January 2023, through both Jordan Outreach Center, and Kingdom United Fellowship, the latter, she has been blessed to serve with since 2022. She has a heart for youth, intercession, worship, and loves to see people meet their surrendered potential. She is the Founding Visionary of Beautiful Spread, which provides hygiene items as well as other necessities to those less fortunate, and is inspired by the scripture in Isaiah 52:1-10 and Revelation 19:9. She currently works as a Licensed Practical Nurse at Charleston Area Medical Center, previously working at that facility as a nursing assistant and patient safety attendant.

She enjoys spending time with the Lord, road trips, hiking, ministering in dance, good food, good phone calls and spending time with the important people in her life. Her favorite passages of scripture are Judges 19:1-20:7 and Psalm 94:17-19.

CHAPTER 9
Forgiving Them Who Hurt You And They Never Knew
By Pastor Kathy Clark

One of the greatest things the Lord told me when someone had hurt us (my husband and me) was to forgive them quickly. Even with tears in our eyes and running down our faces, having just happened and still in our truck driving from the place of hurt, these words kept echoing in my spirit and then in my soul. Forgive them quickly."

13 Be even-tempered, content with second place, quick to forgive an offense. Forgive as quickly and completely as the Master forgave you.
14 And regardless of what else you put on, wear love. It's your basic, all-purpose garment.
Colossians 3:13-14 MSG

When you have been hurt by someone that you respected and served and been a friend to someone and***** has been a sister and brother to the family to the best of your ability, it hurts. The worst is they never knew you were hurting.

You have to continue your life as if it's ok, and the best phase we use is, "I am blessed doing find," and all the while, we are hurting and really want to take matters into our own hands.

I was going to do that, take matters into my own hands, not my husband. I had driven to a place I thought someone would be, and I was going to confront that person to make me feel better. We always have a plan.

I was in the car waiting, and the spirit of the Lord said. What are you doing? What is this going to accomplish? Why are you here?

I heard myself say to myself, stop it, Kathy.

I heard it plain as day, and I grabbed my steering wheel and tears running down my face, and said I am so sorry, Lord. I started my car, put the gear in drive, and drove home hearing, forgive them quickly; they know not. We always think for the other person or persons. We think we know their thoughts and actions. No, we don't; we cannot think for people or even ourselves. God always has a plan for us.

"For my thoughts are not your thoughts, neither are your ways my ways, saith the LORD."

Our thoughts (theirs and ours) are not God's thoughts and certainly not his ways. Sometimes, people think what they do is right and never think about it again. We sometimes act based on what we feel (as I was going to do). We have to trust God for His way. We must trust God when he tells us something and not let the flesh override the words of the Lord. When we are in this vulnerable state in the process, we have to let our flesh die,

Even though it hurts, we have to trust through the hurt and pain of it all. This is not a good feeling at all, but it is a God moment. A God moment is when it is the time to trust past feelings. So, when I was about to do something stupid that I felt would be right, God stepped in, and it was a God moment.

I was in Walmart a couple of days later, or maybe a week later, and I was getting broccoli. This friend or acquaintance in the Lord walked up to me and just began telling me that the Lord said he saw it all and that he was going to repay us. The person said who it was that did this wrong to us by name. I never said anything to them about it. The Lord always has a way of getting a word to you. I speak to you from this place of hurt; don't take any measures to hurt your process. I would have done something totally wrong trying to make myself feel better (or so I thought).

Little did we know that it was for us, not for them, that they had hurt us. I did not believe that they were cognizant of this. God sends healings to us even before we know, just as a doctor prescribes medicine, as it must be taken several days prior before it takes effect in the healing process. God prescribes to us his word for forgiveness, even before we understand the process that is taking place in our lives (forgiving before understanding it).

From our Childhoods and up, A lot of us have been hurt in different situations in our lives, but people who hurt us:

THEY went on with life-
They went on playing,
They went on going to school (elementary, middle school, and high school)
They cheered beside us,
They played in the band beside us,
They played sports with us (basketball, football, run track, soccer, baseball, etc.)
They coached us,
They were our teachers,
They went to college,
They went on to careers,
They went on with their marriage,
They went on shouting beside us at church,
They went on eating with us,
They went on preaching and
They never knew
THEY HURT US. We had to forgive to be free.

Webster's Dictionary defines forgive as a debt canceled. We have to release ourselves to be free and to have peace.

> *"And the peace of God, which passeth all understanding, shall keep your hearts and minds through Christ Jesus. "*

Peace that goes beyond our finite minds and cannot be understood by us, but it is felt. This peace goes into the areas of our spirit to unlock jail bars that tried to hold us imprisoned by feelings of hurt, rejection, and anger. It was not an overnight wonder that happened to us. It was a process. If you can make it through the process, take it one day at a time, not a few days or a week. We cannot rush the process of peace.

    A person who is hurting themselves can only give out of that place until deliverance comes for that person. The person will continue to hurt until they see it is them and not everyone else. When truth hits a person where they are guilty, it will cause an opening that needs to be exposed to deliverance. I have seen it come out in anger and control. The Lord has to close that opening for that person or persons as He did for us.

    This freedom of peace by forgiving brought to us an understanding of God that you can forgive and go on quickly. The pain that people feel in themselves gives others the prison of hurt by their actions. People put you in this prison only if you let them. God did not let us stay in that prison but caused forgiveness to set us free.

    Jesse, King David's father, never knew how much David was hurt being in the fields, tending sheep, while his brothers got to stay in the house. David kept doing what was required of him, which taught him several things. How to trust God and how to fight alone with God. When he was brought into the house, he was summoned by the way of Samuel, the priest God sent to anoint the next King. Another did not take his position because of where he was located.

I said this to say that where you are will not stop what God has for you.1 Samuel 16:1-13. I know you are asking why we didn't let them know. God told us, "DO NOT OPEN UP WHAT'S BEEN SEALED BY OUR FORGIVENESS."

DON'T BE A STUMBLING BLOCK

Let us not judge one another anymore, but judge this rather: that no man puts a stumbling block or an occasion to fall in his brother's way.
Romans 14:13 KJV

Then said Jesus, Father, forgive them; for they know not what they do. And they parted his raiment, and cast lots.
Luke 23:34 KJV

Jesus forgave us when we knew not what we done to Him. We are to do the same. We have to say THAT over and over, they know not...

I forgave you of the hurt you caused, and you did not know
I forgave you for the hurt to go

I picked up peace so I could be free
I chose these, so I could see
The beautiful place of freedom God had for me

Forgive today because when tomorrow comes, it is today.
Forgiveness is for us TODAY
Give ourselves that GIFT...

"For with what judgment ye judge, ye shall be judged: and with what measure ye mete, it shall be measured to you again. "

We have to be careful of the limitations that can come our way from our forgiveness towards others.
I forgive them, but...
Don't let that limit you from reaping a short measure for yourself.

Forgive us, for we know not...
What about when we hurt someone and we do not know what we did? Oh, it's different when it is us, right.
No, ma'am, no sir, it is not...
What you give out will come back.
We are so quick to forget or judge differently when we are wearing the shoe at fault.
We also say I forgive, but don't forget, no ma'am, no sir, forgive and forget. God does not remember what we have done, but we want to put our own reasoning on the matter:

I will forgive but not forget
I will forgive, but we are not going to tea
I will forgive, but I will never let that person back in, etc.
What if God did not forgive Peter for betraying him? Oh yes, He forgave him because He said, but I have prayed for you. I have a question for you: do you pray for the one that hurt you and doesn't even know? Because Jesus prayed for Peter and us', Father forgives them for they know not...

Be careful not to pull others into our hurt and be just like the ones who hurt us. What we say about the people who hurt us or someone else can cause the people you tell to dislike them (wrong). Keep your mouth shut. When you tell the truth, sometimes it can get you in trouble with the Lord.

"Whoso keepeth his mouth and his tongue keepeth his soul from troubles."
Proverbs 21:23

Don't put them in your prison with you.
Please, ma'am, and please, sir, have the gift of shut up. Words have power. What you tell somebody travels and can produce a negative effect

"Death and life are in the power of the tongue: And they that love it shall eat the fruit thereof. "

It did not say a saved man or woman. It said the tongue, meaning every tongue, everyone.

Who do you forgive? If you did not know it caused harm to you, God will forgive you of those you caused harm to...

"To whom ye forgive anything, I forgive also: for if I forgave anything, to whom I forgave it, for your sakes forgave I it in the person of Christ; lest Satan should get an advantage of us: for we are not ignorant of his devices. "

Forgive forgive and forgive again.
So, that God can forgive and forgive you again and again

7 Be not deceived; God is not mocked: for whatsoever a man soweth, that shall he also reap.

8 For he that soweth to his flesh shall of the flesh reap corruption; but he that soweth to the Spirit shall of the Spirit reap life everlasting.

9 And let us not be weary in well doing: for in due season we shall reap, if we faint not.

Galatians 6:7-9 KJV

Sow the seed of forgiveness to those who did not know of the wrong to you. Reap the seed of forgiveness from those you hurt, and you did not know.

PASTOR KATHY CLARK

Kathy Clark

Kathy Clark was born in the beautiful mountains of Charleston West Virginia, She was raised in the church from a young age, by the inspiration of her mother, the late, Mother Mildred Wood. She later accepted Jesus at a young age in a little Baptist church in Montgomery. She later was moved by God from an indept study of scriptures to join Bishop T D Jakes ministry in 1981. God began to open up more revelation after she was baptized in the Holy Ghost, with the evidence of speaking in an unknown tongue.

She has attended Shinning Light and Abundant Life Colleges in Charleston, WV, where she is two classes away from her Bachelor's degree in Theology. She retired from Verizon Telephone Company after 30 years in 2005.

She accepted God's call to pastor Lion Of Judah International Ministry in 2017 with her husband, Elder Jeff Clark. She also has a women's ministry, Gathering Of The Esthers (GOTE), where men and women are set free from the devil.

She enjoys seeing people move in the gifts and callings of God.

She and her husband, Jeffrey serve together to destroy the very work of the enemy. They have two children, Deanna and Kaleb and three grandchildren and one great grandchild.

CHAPTER 10
The Miracle of Forgiving
By Pastor Roslyn Williams

In your lifetime, you will meet many people, and they will come and go in and out of your life. Some will be acquaintances, some you'll have somewhat of a friendship, and some will become what you consider to be a lifelong friend. After a while, you begin to believe this is someone I'll be close with, someone I'll always be able to laugh with, cry with, be mad with, be truthful with, remove all barriers, and be completely open with them no matter what is going on in my life, but life doesn't always work out like that. Situations and circumstances can arise that cause a breach in a friendship you thought would always be there, and you experience a sense of hurt, betrayal, and unforgiveness. These are feelings you never thought you would have toward the person you called friend.

This happened to me, and it was so easy to shut down when that situation arose. Instead of allowing the love of God and forgiveness to overtake the situation quickly, I built a fortress of offense, which then became a fortress of defense, which had very tall walls built around it because I was determined never to allow anyone in my personal space. I was never going to become close with anyone else, not realizing that that wall was not only keeping people out, but it was also keeping God out. I didn't understand that unforgiveness is a breeding ground for bitterness; unforgiveness convinces you that you're right in everything you feel, no matter how bad the thoughts or the words may be. I never took a minute to think about how I was disappointing the Lord with my actions because, if the truth be told, I liked being in that angry place and could justify every thought I had and every word I spoke because "I'm the victim." I will never forgive them for causing me to feel this way.

Matthew 6:14-15 For if you forgive men their trespasses, your Heavenly Father will also forgive you: but if you do not forgive others their trespasses, neither will your Father forgive your trespasses.

This scripture tells us that it is imperative for us to forgive, if we expect the Father to forgive us, and we need to be forgiven daily. Unforgiveness is meant to bring nothing but destruction to your life. It is a weapon the enemy uses to bring separation between you and your Heavenly Father.

After living in unforgiveness for well over a year but still professing to love the Lord with all my heart, a situation arose in my life, and I needed a manifested miracle in my life. As I cried out to God one day, I clearly heard Him say apologize. I didn't call anyone to ask what they thought, I didn't question God, I didn't put any thought into the apology, I picked up the phone, made the call, and allowed the Holy Ghost to speak. Not only did I apologize, but I was able to thank them for some things that took place over the years.

You may say I will never apologize to someone who hurt me until they apologize first, but when you hear the voice of God clearly and understand that (1 Samuel 15:22) says obedience is better than sacrifice and come to the realization that you are not perfect, that you have said things and done things to people that may have hurt their feelings, caused them to shrink back and build a fortress. God forgave you, how can you possibly continue to hold on to unforgiveness and what does it get you in the end?

Colossians 3:13 Be even tempered, content with second place, quick to forgive an offense.

When disagreements happen in your life, make a conscious decision to obey the word of the Lord and forgive quickly. Understand that forgiving does not make you weak; it simply means you are willing to put what you think and how you feel on the back burner and follow the instructions of the Father.

Giving an apology changed my heart position. I went from being angry to being humbled. I believe because I obeyed the spirit of the Lord and did not try to plead my case and convince Him that I had every right to feel the way I did, two miracles took place in my life. A physical and emotional healing and reconciliation of a friendship I thought could never be restored. If we would get our flesh out of the way, forgive, and repent quickly, I believe it would open doors for many miracles to manifest in our lives.

Forgiveness is the key that unlocks the door for a person to be healed and set free from the thoughts and feelings that the enemy sends to be a constant reminder of what took place that caused you to be hurt. It takes away his power to torment you when the person who hurt you walks into the same room you're in. Forgiveness allows you to breathe again and put yourself in a position to be able to open yourself up to other people whom God may send to speak life, healing, and deliverance to you. Forgiveness opens the door for you to have the Joy of the Lord flowing in your life and brings reconciliation that you thought would never be possible.

Micah 7:18-19 (NIV) Who is a God like you, who pardons sin and forgives the transgression of thee remnant of his inheritance? You do not stay angry forever but delight to show mercy.

You will again have compassion on us; you will tread our sins underfoot and hurl all our iniquities into the depths of the sea.

Can you imagine how many times in your "SAVED" Life God has forgiven you and shown you mercy, and never talked about it, never thought about it, and never got mad about it again? I'm sure the times are innumerable. So why is it that we choose to continue to be mad about something that happened 20 – 30 years ago and refuse to forgive? If you choose not to forgive, and it is a choice, the Father will not forgive you. Ask yourself if the offense that happened is worth your salvation. Is it worth being angry all the time, and you can't even remember exactly what happened or when?

Don't allow your flesh to keep you in a place of misery, hatred, and anger. Why take a chance to miss the opportunity to be in the presence of God simply because you would not forgive? Make a conscious decision to forgive all things, and not only forgive but apologize to the person for the thoughts that you have had about them, for the words that you have spoken about them, for the way that you have felt about them. Our lives should always exemplify Christ no matter what.

Prayer

Father, in the name of Jesus, I come to you on behalf of every person reading this who may be overtaken by a spirit of unforgiveness. I pray that the love of God goes in and begins to heal every hurt and place of offense in their lives. Let every wounded place heal completely, and let a true spirit of forgiveness and love overtake their lives. I decree and declare in the name of Jesus that every thought and feeling that has held them captive in unforgiveness will be broken off their lives, and restoration of every God-ordained relationship will manifest in their lives.

Teach us how to forgive quickly, teach us how to love unconditionally, and let us show the Love of God to each person we come in contact with and the enemy of unforgiveness that they see today; they will see no more in Jesus' Name. Amen

Pastor Roslyn Williams

Pastor Roslyn Williams is the Pastor of King of Glory International ministries in Charleston WV under the Apostolic covering of Apostle Tina M Beatty Senior Pastor.

Her ministry was birthed from Luke 4: 18 which explains her passion for seeing believers healed, delivered and set free through the power of God to fulfill their God-given purpose and destiny on this earth.

She is anointed with a strong clear prophetic voice that is evident in the ministry of deliverance, teaching, preaching and intercession which is demonstrated through her fiery expression as she brings forth the word of God in the US as well as internationally.

Her brand of See Yourself On The Other Side was birthed during one of the hardest times in her life, but God was faithful to bring total healing and see her through to the other side where victory was waiting. She is also a certified Life Coach, and always directs her client to the wonder working Power of the Lord. Transformation Apostolic Ministries WV is a ministry originated in North Carolina Under the Apostolic covering of Apostle Gloria McDuffey designed to bring transformation into believers' lives.

Pastor Roz as she is affectionately called, has been happily married to her husband Kenneth for 30 years, she is the mother of three children and has nine beautiful grandchildren.

CHAPTER 11
To Forgive Or Not To Forgive?
By Tunisia K. Beatty

Throughout my darkest moments, with hate in my heart, bitterness in my bones, anger in my soul, and revenge on my mind. After being hurt time after time, I began to ask God why. It just didn't seem fair, and I was destined for answers. Whether or not I'd like what I discovered, I really didn't care at the time. I had gotten to a point in my life where I felt like I'd been chewed up, spit out, and walked over a million times. Life was getting the best of me. It's not just one particular thing that I'm speaking of. Life has handed me my share of lemons, and I've dealt with most of them accordingly.

There have been situations full of hurt, resentment, hostility, disloyalty, pain, and disappointments throughout my life. And I'm not saying I've never been on the other side of that fence because I'm not perfect. For instance, I've suffered from church hurt at the hands of loved ones. This is never an easy thing to deal with. Because it's the Lord's house, I didn't expect these types of things to occur. Church families are supposed to love, trust, and care for one another. But I realized that we are all still human. Sometimes, I expect the unexpected so I don't leave too much room for disappointment. I had to learn to be upset with the spirit and not the person, even though it took a while for me to get to that point.

There have been times when I've been let down by the police, who are supposed to protect and serve. This was an unfortunate situation, but it made it extremely hard for me to trust them at the end of the day. But God had to work on me and adjust my perspective regarding the law. Many professionals in the medical field have let me down, and I've been in some life-or-death situations. I had to pray a lot in order for me or my children to be able to go in for a checkup. And yes, I know that all law enforcement and all physicians aren't the same. But when your life is in someone else's hands, and their decisions determine your outcome, it's a different ball game.

I have been through my share of sexual abuse and molestation. This is not something that many people know about me. But I'm choosing to be transparent on this platform just to show the true strength of forgiveness. Being touched on and fondled as a young child can be detrimental. I've been neighbors with my abusers. And to this day, when I see them, I can look them straight in their eyes and speak without any ill will towards them. God has revealed to me that it was the spirit within them that harmed me.

There was this time when I was only a teenager and I was assaulted while getting my nails done by a grown man. I was followed by him and pulled into a hallway. This was a really dark time in my life, where I began to hate men completely. Even later in my life, having to deal with also being a rape victim. I had so many thoughts running through my head. I would ask myself over and over if it was my fault. Did I not say "No" or "Stop" loud enough? Could I have fought harder or even screamed louder? I was ashamed to even speak about what had happened.

I was so embarrassed (even though I was a victim) that I never even reported it. And I know that God was right there with me because I'm a living testimony, and I'm able to speak out about it now. I'm not saying that those thoughts of my past don't arise from time to time. But I'm so happy I was delivered, healed, and free from those unfortunate experiences.

Then, I had the chapters of my life where I had to deal with lies, deception, mental, spiritual, and physical abuse. Then, I had the chapters of my life where I had to deal with lies, deception, mental, spiritual, and physical abuse. These were the chapters of my life that I dealt with, and I liked to call them "The Takers!" During this time, I was very vulnerable and easily taken advantage of. Even though I had to learn the hard way and my feelings were hurt, I managed to make it. I was just so confused about how to be so good to those I loved, yet I continued to be treated badly.

Every day, I prayed for a change in not only their souls but mine as well. I was eager to love them unconditionally, but the anger and hate deep down in my soul wouldn't allow me to do so. My negative thoughts and my nightmares consumed me. I wasn't sleeping well in fear of what would happen next. I was afraid to lose my life or to take it. But God reminded me that I've got so much to live for, including my babies. I tried to hide my pain deep down inside while keeping a smile on my face. Fake it until you make it, they say, but I wasn't fooling anybody. My scars were so deep from the inside out. One day, I got fed up with everybody taking my kindness for a weakness, and I began fighting back. It didn't make things better, but at the time, it made me feel better.

I got tired of just letting "Life" beat me down! Some people will get you in that mental space where you just feel so worthless. I felt like a failure, and I couldn't find myself. But I'm stronger today because of what I went through, and I give all thanks to God! But during my season of healing and deliverance, I've also hurt others in the process. I can admit that it wasn't right for me to treat others like I did.

I pushed my loved ones away out of anger. And that saying is very true: hurt people do hurt others. I'm a living testimony of that. I began to put up a wall and was bitter to the core, with a hard shell that enclosed me. I started to believe I was gonna get them before they got me. My guard was up, and it was hard to get down. I felt as though I needed to protect myself by any means necessary. I became depressed, I had low self-esteem, I felt like a failure, and I had negative thoughts. I was so low that I felt unworthy of being loved. I didn't even love myself, making it almost impossible to love anyone else. I barely managed to get through the days.

I began to ask myself, "To Forgive or Not To Forgive?" And God replied, "Would you rather be right, or would you rather be happy?" I had to develop the power of forgiveness because it wasn't in me. It was most definitely a process, and it didn't happen overnight. I must admit that I still have days where I struggle. The devil will try to get in my mind and have me reminisce about that past hurt. I had been hurt so badly that I turned into someone that I didn't recognize. I would look at myself in the mirror in disgust.

Forgiveness can have some powerful health benefits. It released me of the control the people who wronged me had over my life. Forgiveness allowed me to move forward. I then began to understand that forgiveness wasn't for them but for me! I needed to do this for my health, my sanity, my children, my family, and our well-being. It was never just about me because I was being selfish. Our futures depended on my forgiveness. It didn't mean that I was forgetting or excusing the harm that was done to me. My flesh was scarred, but my spirit was willing. I had to forgive to get my life back! And just as God forgives me daily, I, too, have to do the same. When I was able to say to God, "Thank You for my experiences," I knew it was real because forgiveness is a lifestyle!

TUNISIA K. BEATTY

FAMOUS QUOTES ON FORGIVENESS

"We must develop and maintain the capacity to forgive. He who is devoid of the power to forgive is devoid of the power to love."
-Martin Luther King Jr.

"It's not an easy journey to get to a place where you forgive people. But it is such a powerful place because it frees you."
~Tyler Perry
To Forgive Or Not To Forgive?
By Tunisia K. Beatty

They say, free yourself and the rest shall follow,
Forgiveness may sound like an easy task, but it's a hard pill to swallow,
After feeling so low, like you've been chewed up and spit out a million times over,
You just try to keep the peace, lay low, and not give everyone the cold shoulder,
Your intentions aren't to be rude or push anyone away,
But after the repetitive disappointments, there's not much more left to say...
Things tend to get old, weigh you down, and you begin to resent so much,
You start to get angry, hateful, bitter, and begin using it all as a crutch,

At the end of the day, there's no justification for your actions,
You start to question God and wonder why this all had to happen,
He reveals the truth right before your eyes,
But it's not the answer you were seeking, so you continue to sulk and despise,
Then one day, you realize that God has forgiven you for all of the sins that you've committed,
You too have lied, cheated, been disloyal, arrogant, evil and hurtful whether or not you want to admit it,
Forgiveness isn't easy, but it can be done...
It's most definitely a process, and trust me, you won't be the first one,
Forgive all who have wronged you, not for them, but for yourself,
It will eliminate stress, heartache, sleepless nights, and better your health...
You'll thank yourself in the end because you'll be able to genuinely love, smile and live...
So, the question of the hour is... "TO FORGIVE OR NOT TO FORGIVE?"

(Poem by: Tunisia K. Beatty)

Tunisia K. Beatty

Tunisia K. Beatty was born and raised in the Wild and Wonderful Charleston, WV. She's currently a Licensed Cosmetologist at Nappy by Nature, with many talents and hobbies. She enjoys writing poetry, painting, drawing, photography, basketball, modeling, and spending quality time with her family. She is the proud mother of five lovely children, whom she loves dearly. They keep her grounded and motivated every day.

Tunisia is also a very educated woman. She graduated from St. Albans High School in 2002, then went on to graduate from West Virginia State University (WVSU) and West Virginia State Community and Technical College (WVSCTC) in 2006. She received an Associate's Degree in Science (Pre-Nursing option), a Medical Coding Certificate & a Paraprofessional Educator Certificate.

After that, just to shake things up, she continued her education after college by completing a Cosmetology program at Carver, a Certified Nursing Assistant (CNA) program at Garnet Career Center, a Medical Assistant (MA) program at ROSS, and also studied some Nuclear Medicine at BridgeValley Community and Technical College.

You can connect with Tunisia via email at
kamece2003@yahoo.com

CHAPTER 12
I Have Forgiven You
By Norma Nanette Hines

Can you imagine growing up in an emotionally, physically, and psychologically abusive home? There was a falsehood about the way my home was established. My parents had a relationship with God, and this was the image displayed in front of others, but it was a different story behind closed doors. Because on the outside, they lived one way, and on the inside (inside of our home), they lived another way.

Those who were around me and my family daily seemed like a "happy family," but a lot was going on that others didn't know about. It caused me to be in bondage that I didn't recognize because, growing up, I was made fun of and belittled in so many ways, which caused me to start second-guessing myself, questioning people's motives, and having trust issues.

The rejection caused the root of these feelings I felt coming from my father. I carried moments of disappointment and heavy burdens that were not meant for me to carry. I was paralyzed with fear and dealt with low self-esteem. These experiences I encountered as a child grew up with me in different areas of my life. And it made me feel betrayed and ostracized by the man I called "Daddy."

For many years, I watched my mother live in fear, and sometimes, in life, we were faced with decisions that occurred in the face of death. I later learned that my mother, who was an Evangelist, would pray daily with her prayer partner for me and my siblings because of what we were experiencing, even though she, too, was going through it as well.

She was a God-fearing mother who was the glue that held the family together. I never understood why my mother chose to stay in this relationship. Despite the many things I endured growing up, I knew it had to be the Lord and my mother's prayers that helped me excel academically and make a "happy family" for myself, different from what I grew up in. At different times in my life, I learned lessons about forgiveness.

To *forgive* means to stop blaming or being mad at someone for something that person has done, or not punish them for something[1]. And *forgiveness* means the act of forgiving[2].

Forgiveness is not a feeling - it's a decision we make because we want to do what's right before God. It's a quality decision that won't be easy, and it may take time to get through the process, depending on the severity of the offense. ~ Joyce Meyer

---

[1] https://dictionary.cambridge.org/us/dictionary/english/forgive

[2] www.merriam-webster.com/dictionary/forgiveness

Forgiveness has the power to mend broken relationships, heal deep wounds, set every soul free from the shackles of bitterness, resentment and anger such as what we experienced in our family. Forgiveness is a courageous act that can bring about inner peace, allowing individuals to let go of the past and embrace a future filled with hope, love, restoration, and reconciliation. As you continue to read my testimony, you see how the power of forgiveness worked in my life and is still working in my life.

We think that forgiveness is weakness, but it's absolutely not; it takes a very strong person to forgive.
~ T. D. Jakes

I think the first step is to understand that forgiveness does not exonerate the perpetrator. Forgiveness liberates the victim. It's a gift you give yourself.
~ T. D. Jakes

My forgiveness story,
As I sat at a homegoing celebration on a Saturday morning, I received a call from the hospital. I was informed that my father would be moving to hospice care. I immediately felt, "This is it," and left the service I was in.

A feeling of loneliness came over me as the thought crossed my mind about how I would feel having both parents deceased. Once I arrived at the facility, I informed the staff of who I was. I was given a pamphlet on the stages of dying. It was an overwhelming feeling. I learned that being the oldest child, the task would fall to me to sign the body over to the funeral home once he was deceased. I also learned that no nourishment, medication, or intravenous fluids would be given. I kept thinking this is it; it is really happening.

As the day went on, I took small steps to receive all this information all at once. After being at the facility all day, I decided to leave at nightfall. The Bible teaches us to *"Honor thy father and thy mother: that thy days may be long upon the land which the Lord thy God giveth thee"* Exodus 20:12 KJV. Despite everything, I wanted to honor my father. It was important to be a good example for my younger siblings. I had always obeyed my parents even when I didn't want to.

Before I left the facility for the evening, I asked God, "What do you want me to do?"

Everyone was at work, and at this moment, it was my father, God, and myself. I turned my face to the wall, and God told me to "forgive" him (my father) for what he had done and that it would be finished. I walked over to the bed, bent over, and whispered in his ear, "Daddy, WE FORGIVE YOU. Go ahead and leave; we will be fine, and we will do good in life. You can go."

My mind was immediately flooded with some memories that should never have been seen or heard. The many negative comments he would utter to us, but we, as his children, tried to love him anyway.

"...And be ye kind one to another, tenderhearted, forgiving one another, even as God for Christ's sake hath forgiven you." (Ephesians 4:32 KJV)

Immediately, his breath left his mouth and went to his throat. I saw this change right before my eyes, and I believe God gave me this because I was the oldest child. I noticed a nurse leaving the room across the hall, and I asked her to come into the room where I was with my father to see if he was still breathing because of what I saw happening to him.

The nurse said, "Yes, he's leaving us," she started to time his breath with her watch. This was like at 3:45 pm, she got her stethoscope and checked certain points, and by 3:50 pm, she said, "He's gone." "Death and life are in the power of the tongue: and they that love it shall eat the fruit thereof." (Proverbs 18:21 KJV).

I was overwhelmed with tears, thinking about what I had just said to my father as I obeyed God, doing exactly what He told me to do. I wasn't expecting that, But God knew what was needed for the end of his story and the new beginning for my siblings by reassuring my father to transition, and it happened.

As I continued to cry, I realized at that moment how powerful forgiveness was and my obedience in my father's death and in our family. In spite of what took place in our family growing up, God knew what was needed before he took his last breath.

"Servants, obey in all things your masters according to the flesh; not with eyeservice, as menpleasers; but in

singleness of heart, fearing God; And whatsoever ye do, do it heartily, as to the Lord, and not unto men; Knowing that of the Lord ye shall receive the reward of the inheritance: for ye serve the Lord Christ."
(Colossians 3:22-24 KJV)

As the thought came back to me earlier of being without my parents is now my reality. Even though my relationship with my father had been strained, he was still my father. In adulthood, I now process grief in ways I didn't understand in prior years when I faced immediate loss. My grief was delayed because of my fear of being alone and shocked that I was now alone after the passing of both of my parents. With God's grace, I was able to let him know he was forgiven. I wonder if this was what he was holding on for. Only God knows. But the nurse stood right there with me and made sure I was all right, and I'm thankful for that.

"Peace I leave with you, my peace I give unto you: Not as the world giveth, give I unto you. Let not your heart be troubled, neither let it be afraid."
(John 14:27 KJV)

I would soon start to feel the loneliness in my heart in the days, weeks, and months ahead. The family unit, as I once knew it, was no longer there. I would have never imagined I would be able to release my father with forgiveness. Even in death, I will honor my parents, and I did what was necessary for myself and my siblings. I was reminded that difficult roads lead to beautiful destinations. *"And when ye stand praying, forgive, if ye have ought against any; that your father also which is in heaven may forgive you your trespasses"* (Mark 11:25 KJV). This scripture compelled me to forgive because of the unforgiveness in my heart towards my father.

Unforgiveness is a grudge against someone who has offended you. Another definition of unforgiveness is not having the compassion to forgive. Unforgiveness is a sin that causes us to think and do evil things. If someone has offended us, we have a choice to either forgive them or not forgive them. When we choose not to have compassion for someone who has offended us, and we choose not to have the willingness to forgive them. Matthew 18:33 advises us to have compassion for our fellow man as God has had mercy on us.[3]"

So I believe God is pleased with my decision to forgive but most of all, my obedience to what He told me to do because it could have gone another way, meaning I might not would have had the opportunity again to let him know that I forgive him. And this would have bothered me, knowing I had a chance to tell him, but I didn't. BUT GOD KNEW!!! And I'm so grateful, forgive, and live that abundant life God has for you.

It's important to recognize that forgiveness is more than mere words; it's a heart attitude that induces a spiritual transformation.
~ Victoria Osteen

---

[3] christcenteredhouseofgod.org

Through this process, I am still learning lessons on forgiveness, but I am determined not to let anything or anybody change the outlook I have on life because God has been so good to me. Forgiveness is a part of my daily bread...*After this manner, therefore pray ye: Our Father which art in heaven, Hallowed be thy name. Thy kingdom come, Thy will be done in earth, as it is in heaven. Give us this day our daily bread. And forgive us our debts, as we forgive our debtors. And lead us not into temptation, but deliver us from evil: For thine is the kingdom, and the power, and the glory, forever. Amen.* (Matthew 6:9-13 KJV)

My main purpose is for individuals to grab hold of forgiveness and to realize you are way better than unforgiveness in every area of your life. Forgive Father, Mother, Brother, Sister, Family. Whoever needs forgiveness, forgive them. Forgiveness will deliver and heal you in every area of your life. *Isaiah 53:11 KJV But he was wounded for our transgressions, he was bruised for our iniquities: the chastisement of our peace was upon him; and with his stripes we are healed.* We got this, ya'll, because God has got us in the palm of his hand. We are the clay, and you already know he is the potter molding and making us after he will. Does it hurt? Yes, it does! But God, with pressure being applied, we shall come forth as pure gold, having been tried in the fire.

In order to move to the next level of elevation in God, we all must forgive, especially when we know that it has become a stumbling block in our life. It has become something that consumes our time, causing us to have negative thoughts about what took place. Let's just name it a stronghold. A stronghold because you rehearse over and over a situation or circumstance. Always remember that forgiveness frees you, and you are no longer a slave or bound by a circumstance or a situation. It frees your mind, spirit, and soul.

    I have forgiven him, and God has forgiven me; I am Free, Praise the Lord, I'm Free!

Acronym For Forgiveness:

F - Freedom: Forgiveness grants you the freedom from the burden of resentment and anger.
O - Opportunity: Forgiveness opens the door to new opportunities for growth and healing.
R - Release: Forgiveness allows you to release the hurt and pain so you can move forward.
G - Grace: Forgiveness is an act of grace towards yourself and others.
I - Inner peace: Forgiveness brings inner peace and comfort.
V - Victory: Forgiveness is a triumph over bitterness and resentment.
E - Empowerment: Forgiveness empowers you to live again.

Norma Nanette Hines

Nanette graduated from Dupont High School in 1978. She continued her education and holds an Apprenticeship for Childhood Development Specialist (ACDS) Certification. She is an Autism Mentor through Marshall University Autism Program. Nanette earned her Regents Bachelor of Arts (RBA) at an HBCU, West Virginia State University. She birthed "Testimony Tuesday" via Facebook to encourage herself and others. She is also a proud member and mediator of the Beautiful Soul Sunday Facebook Page. In addition, she is Co- Author of I Live To Tell It Testimonial Anthology- Bestseller and International Bestseller, Co-Author of "I Live To Tell It 'The Power Of Forgiveness" Volume 2 and lastly Author of Nobody But God Journal.

She is a faithful member of her local church, where she serves God. Her favorite saying is, "There is nothing too hard for God." She volunteers on the Essentials Milk and Bread Giveaway Team, Prayer Team, and the Intercessory Prayer Team.

Contact Information:
Email: diamondnailla@aol.com
Facebook: Nanette Hines

CHAPTER 13
The Voice

By Nichelle A. Triggs Robinson

Forgiveness oftentimes comes at a price. The cost can be that which seems unattainable and most definitely intangible. The beauty of forgiveness is that it benefits the person who was hurt, offended, abused, or even mistreated. Of course, we know that as Christians, the Lord requires us to forgive as he forgives us, but we also know that the spirit is willing, but our flesh is weak. Finding my voice to write this chapter was challenging since I faced the very tenants of forgiveness during this writing process.

Recently, I was hurt, mistreated, and lied to, and my heart was stepped on by women that I truly loved, served, and honored in the way God intended me to do. Ironically, I could forgive them quickly, but the giant I faced was much bigger than any of their words or misdeeds. See, forgiveness for me had to start with ME!! I had to forgive myself for many years of critical and analytical thinking of myself.

As I discussed the details of the assault with people that I know love and trust me, I tried to reason with them about what I could have possibly done to deserve this mistreatment. None of them could give me an answer, allowing me to take ownership of this attack. They each encouraged me, and I realized they were right. I am far too critical of myself, and even still, I wanted to take this burden on my back and justify how my offenders had a reason to despise me.

This has been the symphony of my life. It is the song that plays loudly and often. I prefer to avoid confrontation, internalize my pain, and let my negative thoughts of myself speak louder than the power that is within me. There have been multiple areas in my life that include poor decisions in intimate sexual relationships, addictions, horrible communication errors, missteps in birthing opportunities, and this list goes on. All the things of my past that God has forgiven me for still haunted me. Once I concluded that I am the righteousness of God, not because I am righteous but simply because he proclaimed that over my life, and like the young people say, He is "STANDING ON BUSINESS"! I had to fast, pray, counsel, and fight for the ability to forgive myself.

Most people think that being a perfectionist is something that serves them well. That is the polar opposite truth. Perfectionism is rooted in pride, and there lies the area of my life that caused me tremendous pain. Perfectionism is when you try at all costs never to make a mistake or be criticized, which is an unreasonable expectation of yourself. One of the co-authors of this book, who happens to be a close relative, my Pastor, and others were instrumental in allowing me to forgive myself and move on with the greatness that God has placed in me.

Let me offer you some solutions to the most challenging things for me to overcome. As a child, I received so much love, and I was cherished by the people God chose to raise me. At the tender age of 5, I could chug down half a can of Rolling Rock beer when I was asked to grab a cold one from the refrigerator. At the time, it seemed funny, and no one thought it was harmful. But that very thing led me to be a functional alcoholic and a hot mess in my teenage and young adult years. I was convinced that because I had a family history of drinking, this was my portion in life. I met the Lord for real at 35 years old, and one of the deacon's wives at my church prayed a miraculous prayer over me, and I was delivered from that addiction.

I was newly saved, loved The Lord with all my heart, and hadn't had a drink for more than ten years. Then, all hell broke loose in my marriage, and I found myself turning back to what I thought would bring me peace. It took me more than five years to get over that part of my life while I was also living in sin with a man I thought would be my second husband. ALL FAILS! To overcome this addiction, I had to admit it to myself.

My children, who for the most of their lives, never knew about the addictions that were right behind my bedroom door. The addiction caused mood swings, outbreaks of anger, and misplaced aggression towards them. I had to make a continuous decision to break that chain. God once again delivered me through fasting, prayer, and supplication, but there was so much damage done. This led to regret, damnation, and thoughts of suicide. But the one thing that is true in my life is I love my children too much to leave them alone.

Now, let's take a step back and talk about what people will do for money. By people, I mean me! I had a demented mindset when it came to how I interacted in my sexual life that would net a profit that was worth absolutely NOTHING! Yes, there were designer clothes, handbags, respect from others, and fine jewelry, but the price of sin is deadly! I had to realize that while I was never a promiscuous woman, I was a low-down, dirty mess.

I was someone who used abortion as birth control; I was a verbal bully who would most likely become ostracized and isolate myself from There lies a five-dollar hoe that thought she had life figured out but was fastly trending as another statistic. When I had my eldest son – not a saved woman – I was in my room enjoying Trinity Broadcast Network, which was comic relief for me in my foolishness. Then, the enemy tormented my mind. I saw tickers at the bottom of the TV that stated horrible things about me that were tangible. Those words resonated in my soul. The words included that I would be a horrible mom, I was a poor, confused, ratchet woman, I was a home wrecker, and unworthy of God's love.

WHOA!! Writing these truths brings tears to my eyes, but the grace of God is sufficient. That night, I asked God to please allow me to be a great mother to my firstborn son. Despite anything else in my life, I just wanted to be a good mother. I denounced my desire to be a dope dealer's girl, denounced my desire to do anything for money, and I rested in the word that a broken and contrite heart he would not deny. So yes, that is the word of God, but I didn't quite KNOW it at the time.

After the birth of my son, just two short years later, my mother moved to Atlanta to be with me, her only child and her first grandson. I was elated. I was a student at a major university in Atlanta. I was in my own apartment, working a decent job, and I was thriving. Just ten days later, she dropped dead in my bedroom from a pulmonary embolism. WHAT? Yes, *my rock, my friend, my healer, and my savior* was gone. JUST LIKE THAT! Put a pin here because these words were why God would illuminate His importance in my life.

My mother was a very spiritual woman. She followed the faith of Yoruba, and by my account, she was a good human. I don't know much about that faith, but I was exposed to it intimately. However, based on my current faith and beliefs, it was contrary to the way God intended me to live my life. I have many accounts of the good she did for me, but I never accepted that way of life.

As a child, how did I know anything different? I just knew this woman adored me and would never lead me astray. This devastation led me to a very dark place. I argued with God, I was emotionally disconnected from Him, and I believed that He must have cursed me for all the stupid things I did while I was lost and wandering through life as a misfit.

I recall the day before I moved to Atlanta, my mother took me to a "BABA," the name they used in her religion as a priest. That man put razor marks behind my neck, ankles, and wrists. The marks were evident, and if you have ever been seared, you know those marks never fade. However, when I accepted Christ – I mean the very day I was baptized, those marks disappeared. If you look at my body, you will never see evidence of the trauma I experienced.

So, let's look at where I found forgiveness for myself. These things didn't happen to me they happened *for* me. I am a living, breathing testimony that God is my healer, my redeemer, and he loves me beyond my past, present, and future. My healing began once I accepted God, The Father, The Son, and The Holy Ghost. It was not instant. It is still a daily challenge that I contend with and one that provokes me to bear my cross until the day I perish.

I have to fight to bring down strongholds in my life; I have to battle with the voice in my head that tends to remind me of my shortcomings. I also have to remind myself that God forgives us and scatters our sins into an abyss and that He never holds against us, never recollects, and will not place ultimate judgment on us for them. He is faithful to CARE FOR US - not care about us but FOR us, and He will never leave or forsake us. I now rest in God, knowing that the spirit of God lives in me and through me, and I am an overcomer.

The human experience requires tremendous journeys of self-reflection, healing, and spiritual growth. Our willingness to confront our past, acknowledge our mistakes, and seek forgiveness from others and ourselves is a powerful testament to our strength and resilience.

Forgiveness is indeed a complex process that often involves forgiving others but also requires forgiving oneself. The realization that forgiveness has to start with the individual is profound and speaks to the deep inner work we all undertake. My sister writers' stories also highlight the importance of faith and spirituality in our healing journeys. Finding solace and redemption in your relationship with God, despite the challenges and tragedies we have faced, is truly inspiring.

It's evident that the journey toward self-forgiveness is ongoing and may continue to present challenges, but your faith and determination will guide you through. Remembering that God is with you, supporting you, and loving you unconditionally can provide strength and comfort as you navigate the complexities of life.

Thank you, God, for allowing me to share my story with honesty and vulnerability. Our journeys serve as beacons of hope for others who may be struggling with similar challenges, reminding them that healing and forgiveness are possible with faith, perseverance, and self-compassion.

Prayer Of Affirmation

And they overcame him by the blood of the Lamb, and by the word of their testimony; and they love not their lives unto the death.
Revelation 12:11 KJV

BLESS THE Name of THE LORD! Okay, Father, WE DID IT! I thank you for the opportunity to share with the world how you have redeemed me, forgiven me, and provided me with the strength to endure these experiences with you. I am honored that you chose and trusted me to walk out this spiritual transformation with you.

Now, Lord, I pray that as people from every part of the world read this book that testimonies, miraculous healings, and redemption by transformation will come forth. I agree with your word that ALL things work together for good to those who love God and to those who are called according to His purpose (Romans 8:28 NIV).

I pray that every reader realizes that you are a God that answers BIG prayers; you hear every small prayer, every moan, and utterance of tongues. As you present yourself to individuals, I pray that they understand that you are more than understanding, graceful, and merciful to forgive and welcome them unto the holy priesthood.

Father, I leave this affirmation before you and offer it to the readers. I declare that we are healed, whole, and set free by the blood Jesus shed on the cross. AMEN!!

Nichelle A. Triggs Robinson

Nichelle A. Triggs Robinson is a champion for Christ. Born in Youngstown, OH and raised in Inglewood, CA. She currently resides in Atlanta, GA with a wealth of family and friends. She is the co-author of the Anthology - I Lived to Tell It. She is the author of a best selling children's book Integrity which is available on Amazon. She is an intercessor, a current of member of her local church where she has been a member for more than 20 years. Life's challenges may have knocked her down, but the word of God declares: We often suffer, but we are never crushed. Even when we don't know what to do, we NEVER give up. In times of trouble, God is with us, and when we are knocked down, WE GET UP AGAIN!!

2 Corinthians 4:8-9 CEV

31-Day Forgiveness Scripture Plan

Take time and Reflect on each scripture daily to deepen your understanding of forgiveness. Here are 31 scriptures on forgiveness for a daily plan.

1. Matthew 6:14-15
2. Ephesians 4:32
3. Colossians 3:13
4. Luke 17:3-4
5. Psalm 86:5
6. Mark 11:25
7. 1 John 1:9
8. Proverbs 17:9
9. James 5:16
10. Matthew 18:21-22
11. Romans 12:19
12. Ephesians 1:7
13. Isaiah 43:25
14. 1 Peter 3:9
15. Luke 6:37
16. Proverbs 24:17
17. Micah 7:18
18. 2 Chronicles 7:14
19. Acts 3:19
20. Romans 6:23
21. 1 Corinthians 13:4-5
22. 2 Corinthians 2:10
23. Matthew 5:23-24
24. Romans 8:1
25. Psalm 103:12
26. Galatians 6:1
27. Hebrews 8:12
28. Ephesians 4:26-27
29. Isaiah 1:18
30. Proverbs 28:13
31. Colossians 3:14

The How, Why, What, Where, When, and Who to Forgive

How To Forgive:

Forgiving can be challenging, but here are some steps to take:

1. **Acknowledgment of God:** His provision to help us forgive; that's why we seek Him first; we don't have to do it alone.

2. **Understand the Hurt:** Try to understand the perspective of the person who hurt you and forgive if at all possible, and if not, try looking at it from a different point of view to help you overcome the wrong that was done to you.

3. **We Choose to Forgive:** Make a conscious decision to let the resentment go. It is an act of the will. Choose to forgive.

4. **And Release It (Resentment):** Allow yourself to release anything negative that may hinder you from forgiving.

5. **Compassion:** Cultivate compassion for the person who hurt you. This may not be easy to do but it is necessary.

6. **Reflect on Your Own Mistakes:** Understand your own imperfections, forgive and continue

to keep moving. Don't get stuck in your mistakes.

7. **Seek Support If Needed:** Talk to someone you can trust for guidance and support. Someone who believes in what the scripture says about forgiveness. Not one who harbors unforgiveness in their heart because they can't help where they've not been helped. If they don't walk in forgiveness, go find someone else.

8. **Give it Time:** Forgiveness is a process; be patient with yourself and others. But keep seeking God through this process until forgiveness has taken place in your life. It's important that you keep pressing and not give up.

Remember, forgiveness is for your well-being, not necessarily for the person who wronged you.

Why Do You Forgive?

Forgiving is beneficial for several reasons:

1. **Inner Peace:** Letting go of resentment brings a sense of inner peace and tranquility.

2. **Emotional Well-being: Forgiveness** reduces stress, anger, worry, and any negative emotions that come from being overwhelmed by life circumstances.

3. **Health Benefits:** Studies suggest forgiving can positively impact physical health. Forgiving is healing to your soul and can manifest in your physical body.

4. **Relationship Improvement:** Forgiveness fosters healthier relationships and promotes a better understanding of the relationships.

5. **Personal Growth:** It allows you to learn from experiences and grow in every area of your life.

6. **Spiritual Growth:** Many find forgiveness integral to spiritual development in a person's life.

7. **Breaking the Cycle:** It helps break the cycle of negativity, hurt, pain, and memory recall of the

past that keeps coming back up and promotes a renewed mindset, peace of mind, and joy in the Holy Ghost.

8. Because we are commanded by the Word of God to do so!!!

Ultimately, forgiveness is a gift to yourself, offering freedom from the burdens of anger, unforgiveness, bitterness, and resentment.

What To Forgive:

Forgiveness can apply to a range of situations, including:

1. **All Personal Offenses:** Forgiving someone who has hurt or wronged you personally.

2. **All Types of Betrayal:** Forgiving those who have betrayed your trust.

3. **Mistakes:** Forgiving yourself for your own mistakes and shortcomings.

4. **Disagreements:** Forgiving others for differing opinions, misunderstandings, or conflicts.

5. **Past Resentments:** Letting go of grudges and resentments from the past.

6. **Broken Promises:** Forgiving when someone fails to keep their promises.

Essentially, forgiveness is a powerful tool that can be applied in various aspects of life, contributing to emotional well-being and personal growth.

Where To Forgive:

Forgiveness is a process that can happen in various settings:

1. **Prayer Closet:** Praying to God first for forgiveness through prayer

2. **Dialogue:** In some cases, forgiveness may involve open communication with the person involved.

3. **Therapeutic Settings:** Forgiveness can be explored in therapy or counseling sessions.

4. **Writing:** Some find writing about their feelings and the act of forgiveness to be therapeutic.

Remember, forgiveness is a journey that begins with you, and the setting may vary based on timing, personal comfort, and circumstances.

When To Forgive:

The timing of forgiveness varies, but here are some considerations:

1. **Be Ready: Forgiveness** is a personal process and beneficial in every believer's life; do it when you feel like it and do it when you don't feel like it; in the end, you'll be glad you did.

2. **Reflecting on Hurt:** Once you've had time to reflect on the hurt and allowed time to heal, then be led by the Lord for the right timing because God knows.

3. **For Your Well-being:** When holding onto unforgiveness, bitterness, and resentment, it starts affecting your mental, emotional, and physical well-being.

4. **Forgive Again and Again**

5. **Don't Wait on Others:** Forgiveness can happen independently of whether the other person apologizes or changes. Do it for you because it's the right thing to do. There is a quote that said by Prophet Enger Taylor ... Do it even if they are not sorry! That right there speaks volumes.

Forgiving is about your own healing and growth.

Who To Forgive:

1. Everybody
2. Everything
3. Including Yourself

Forgiveness Prayers

Prayer To Forgive Others:

"Dear Lord, grant me the strength to forgive those who have wronged me. Help me to release any bitterness or resentment in my heart. And teach me to love and show mercy, just as You have shown mercy to me. May I reflect Your grace in my interactions with others. In Jesus' name, amen."

Prayer To Forgive Myself:

"Dear Heavenly Father, I come in the name of Jesus Christ; I humbly seek your forgiveness and grace as I forgive myself from sin known and unknown, sin I did willingly or unwillingly. Release me from the burden of guilt and shame. Help me accept your unconditional love and grant me the strength to learn, grow, and move forward in the love and forgiveness you have towards me. In Jesus' name, I pray. Amen."

Forgiveness Prayer For The Wrong I Have Done To Others:

"Dear Heavenly Father, I come in the name of Jesus Christ; I come before you with a repentant heart, acknowledging the wrongs I have done to others. I ask for your forgiveness and mercy. Grant me the strength to make amends and the wisdom to learn from my mistakes. Holy Spirit, lead and guide me in all truth so that I can become a better person by showing forth your love and grace. In Jesus' name, I pray. Amen."

How To Go To Someone And Ask For Forgiveness:

"Lord, as I approach someone seeking forgiveness, guide my words and intentions. Help me to express my sincere repentance, acknowledging the pain I've caused by asking for forgiveness. Grant me the humility to listen and understand their perspective. May your grace be present in this conversation, leading to reconciliation and healing. In Jesus' name, I pray. Amen."

Asking God For Forgiveness:

"Heavenly Father, I humbly come before you in Jesus Christ's name, seeking your forgiveness because of the sin in my life where I missed the mark and fell short of the glory of God. I am asking for your mercy and grace. Cleanse and purge my heart, Lord, and keep me on the straight and narrow path that aligns me to your will being done in my life. Thank you for your unconditional love and the forgiveness found in your boundless compassion. In Jesus' name, I pray. Amen."

Special Thanks

We, the co-authors, want to thank each and every one of you who supported us as a sponsor of this anthology. It is deeply appreciated. Thank you for helping us make a difference in the lives of women and men worldwide.

Alvin and Norma Smith
Andrea Allen
Andre Rogers
Aneica Brooks
Angela Thompson
Angela Spencer
Angela Williams
Angie Franklin
Annette Davis
Anonymous Donor
Anonymous Donor
Apostle Robin Davis
Apostle Roshell Boudreaux
Arya Vanhoose

Barbara Bond - Gentry
Barbara Patterson
Barbara Samuels
Becki and Pete Conley
Bernetta Wood
Betty B. White
Betty Jackson
Betty Poteat
Bishop Bruce King
Bishop Sam R. Calloway Jr. and Pastor Lana Calloway
Bishop TR and Lady Arnise Murray
Bishop Will and Pastor Bonnie Compton
Bonnie McBride
Brenda Joy Hudnall
Brenda McMahon
Brenda Stanley

Brilee Hagan
Brother Antron and Pastor Tia Welch

Carla Ezekiel
Carlotta J Lynch Hospitality LLC
Carol D. Bady
Cecillia House
Cedric and Raquel Greene
Charisa Gary
Christian Jordan
Christina Hines
Christopher, Tiffany, and Alan Brooks
Cindy Burkes
Clark and Christina Lacy

Danielle Lynch Collier
Danielle Wood
Darlene Reynolds
David Releford
Dawntea Ali Cross, Jr.
Deaconess Daines "Cookie" Green
Deanna Wattie
Debra Jones - Stevenson
Debra Schultz
Dee Gazzaway
DeRecco Lynch
Dimitri J. Roach, Jr.
Donna Gilmore - Elzy
Doris Washington - In Loving Memory of Billy Washington
Dorletta Hairston

Dr. Brian Coston
Dr. Frances and Mrs. Tracey Jasmin Fraser
Dr. Lynn Goebel
Dr. Oliver T. Reid
Dr. Sheila Jackson
Dr. Theresa Harris
Dr. Wanda Mann

Ebony Hairston
Eddie and Sylvonne Jordan
Elder Alexis Jones
Elder B. R. King
Elder Frances Banks
Elder Jeff Clark
Elder Pauline Moles
Elder Robin Clark
Elder Roy and Elder Marian Davis
Elder Stacy Murray - Medcalf
Elder Wilbur T. Hines Sr.
Elizabeth Black
Erica McNeil
Eric Wood and Cindy Sea
Erika Law
Erin and Dawntea Cross, Sr.
Esinse Walker
Evangelist Joyce Edwards King
Evangelist Lenora Vance
Evangelist Melissa Flynn
Evelyn Essex

First Lady Denise L. and Rev. Dr. Donald L. Isaac, Sr.

Gail Vannoy
Geraldine Brisco
Geraldine Tibbs
Gloria Hargo
Gloria V. Jordan
Gregory McBride
Gregory and Tonya Edwards
Gretchen Petty

Hamid Sabur
Harriett Handley
Harry McBride
Hayle Martin
Heather M. Francisco
Huey Woodson

I Lived To Tell It, LLC
In Loving Memory of Harold Jackson
In Loving Memory of Kenneth Williams Sr.
In Loving Memory of Mary Frances Brooks
In Loving Memory of Norma Arlene Pierce
In Loving Memory of Prophet Charlene Hines
In Loving Memory of Robert D. Burns
In Loving Memory of Ronald Jackson

Jackie Smith
Jade Smith Lewis
James E. Wiseman
James M. Allen, Sr. (Posthumously)
James A. Jones, Sr.

Jamie Spangler
Janet Johnson - Brewer
Jania Battle
Janice Holland
Jeanette Jackson
Jeff and Robin Namey
Jen Cottrell
Jennifer Hicks
Jennifer Mosley
Jennifer Nettleton
Jennifer Stover
Jessica Mathis
Jessica Nettleton
Jessica Wallace
JetLife Consulting
John Keefers
Joy S. Allen

Kaleb Clark
Kara Lynch Carter
Kathy and Alphonso Jones
Katrina Helm
Kelli Lynch
Keith and Gloria McCullough
Kenneth Williams Jr.
Kenneth and Roslyn Williams 9 grandchildren ~ Asaun Harper, Kameron Genzmer, Abigail Caldwell, Angelo Lacy, Aiden Caldwell, Allahna Lacy, Ariel Jones, Amir Gary, Adonis Lacy
Kim May
King of Glory International Ministries

Kisa Loyd
Kisha Burns
Kiwana Denson
Kori Hargraves

LaTausha Taylor
Lateisha Henry
Lauren S. Haynie
Leah Harris
Leon and Sabith Chisolm
Linda A. Boyer
Linda Fulmer
Linda Wray
Lion of Judah International Ministries
Lisa Perry Bowling
Lois Metz
IottaGod Ministries
Lucinda Mickle
Lydia Shaw
Lynnessa Johnson
Lynn Thompson

Mabel Turner
Mario Denson
Marion Y. Johnson
Mark Anthony Hines
Marti Dolin
Matthew Samuel
Mattie Belle Jordan
Melanie Battle
Melody Jordan

Michael and Carol Brown
Michael and Mary Baldwin
Michael LaMarr
Michele Hannah
Michelle Elkins
Michelle Koren Smith
Michelle R. Wells
Mike McKeny
Minister Shemar Ray
Monica Willis
Monique Curley
Mr. and Mrs. Carl S. Wilson
Myla Searcy

Nakia Austin
Naomi Robinson
Nappy by Nature Salon
Naydene Williams

O'Daylah Vante - Zellous
Opal Revels
Overseer E. Patrick Porter

Pastor Barbara Jones
Pastor Bryan and Pastor Lisa Hagan
Pastor Kathie Holland
Pastor Latoya Martin Ray
Pastor Greg and Pastor Tammy Strader
Pastor Paul Dunn
Pastor Rhobielyn Lewis
Pastor Samantha Salley

Pastor Tim and First Lady Chelsea Davis
Pastor Wanda Shelton
Patricia and Arthur Joseph
Patricia Hagan
Patricia Hines
Peggy Barnett
Penny Jones
Pricilla Doan
Professor Tierra D. Graves
Prophetess Kerry - Ann Wilkinson
Prophet Yvonne Franklin

Rae Caldwell and Robin Alexander
Rachel Barker Toney
Ramon and Andi Bassett
Ramona Fox
Reggie and Pinky Daniels
Regina White - Kirk
Regina Williams
Renea Wood
Reverend Theresa Brown
Rhonda Milton
Rick Mitchell
Rick Workman
Rileigh Phillips
Robin Bonner
Robin Igo
Ronald and Pamela Ross
Ronald C. Beatty
Rosie White

Sandi Flockhart
Samantha Harris
Sami Toler
Sarah Payne
Scot and Shirley Miller
Shamaya Law
Shante Williams
Sharon Gibson
Shawnta Allen Hines
Shay Martin
Sheila Burns
Sheila Mitchell
Shelbee M. Blanks
Shirley Jones Wooding
Simone Lavery
Sonja Almonte
Star Hogan
Stephanie Ramsey
Stephanie Robinson
Stop Violence Against Women
Susan Toliver

Tammy Browning
Tatilia Burroughs
Taylor Ray
Terresa Leonard
Terri Hively
The Beatty Bunch Tunisia, Tiana, Teika, Ronnie Jr. (Taylor), Grandchildren and Bonus Grandchildren
The Bonner Nieces and Great Nieces
Thelma "Suzie" Davis Battle

Theresa Johnson
Tiffanee Jelks
Tiffany Brooks
TMBeatty Ministries Inc.
Tondra Hagerty
Trisha Rizzo
Tyrone Pierce
Valerie Taylor
Vanessa Walker
Vicki L. Pleasant

Wilbur T. Hines Jr.
William C. Morgan
Willie Brooks
Willie C. Tarplin II
Wilma Dixon

Xaviera McFadden

Yolanda F. Brown

#BATTLE4LIFE

Made in the USA
Middletown, DE
17 May 2024